This book first frightens, then entrances as it lays bare the hidden idols of the heart. It entrances with the promise of a treasure worth more than all our idols put together. And ultimately, it liberates with a vision of Christ so compelling and so powerful that the reader says, "O Lord, set me free and I will be free indeed." It's easy to make people feel guilty about their idols. Greg Dutcher inspires us to set aside our trinkets in pursuit of the Ultimate Treasure."

Dr. Ray Pritchard, president of Keep Believing Ministries
and author of *An Anchor for the Soul, The Healing
Power of Forgiveness, He's God and We're Not*

The first two commandments and the cautionary history of ancient Israel should set our hearts at their highest level of alert against idolatry. Perhaps we are more sophisticated than our forefathers who made wood and stone images of their gods—but ours are no less deadly for being invisible. We need to drag them out into the light and smash them to pieces in repentance. Greg Dutcher's book serves as a set of "night-vision goggles" to help us root these insidious idols out of our hearts. Then he goes further and restores and renews us in full-fledged adoration of Jesus.

Kris Lundgaard, author of *The Enemy Within*

Of the making of books that make us feel better there is no end, but books that actually make us better are rare. Greg Dutcher has done the rare thing: journeyed into the heart of darkness—our penchant for idols—and then blazed a trail back into daylight. He dares to tell us the bad news about ourselves in order that we can hear, clear and fresh, the good news in spite of ourselves.

Mark Buchanan, author of *The Rest of God: Restoring
Your Soul by Restoring Sabbath* and *Hidden in Plain Sight*

Greg Dutcher's book is excellent. It is biblical in content and very well written. It is wonderful that Greg has made the subject so accessible. He is a master of illustration. The discussion of the idols of our lives leads to a strong affirmation of the gospel. This book would be great for adult or high school Bible studies or as a gift for an inquirer.

Dr. John Frame, professor of systematic theology and philosophy, Reformed Theological Seminary, and author of *The Doctrine of God* and *Salvation Belongs to the Lord*

This is a great book (and a needed one), and Greg's writing is crisp and fun.

Dr. Steve Brown, nationally syndicated talk-show host, Key Life Network

YOU are the
treasure
that I seek

*But there's
a lot of
cool stuff
out there, Lord

GREG DUTCHER

DISCOVERY HOUSE
PUBLISHERS®

Discovery House Publishers is affiliated with RBC Ministries, Grand Rapids, Michigan.

Requests for permission to quote from this book should be directed to: Permissions Department, Discovery House Publishers, P.O. Box 3566, Grand Rapids, MI 49501 or contact us by e-mail at permissionsdept@dhp.org

All Scripture quotations, unless otherwise indicated, are taken from *The Holy Bible, English Standard Version*. Copyright © 2000; 2001 by Crossway Bibles, a division of Good News Publishers. Used by permission. All rights reserved.

Interior design by Michelle Espinoza

Library of Congress Cataloging-in-Publication Data

Dutcher, Greg, 1970-
You are the treasure that I seek: but there's a lot of cool stuff out there, Lord / Greg Dutcher.
    p. cm.
  ISBN 978-1-57293-309-5
1. God--Worship and love. 2. Spirituality. 3. God (Christianity) 4. Idolatry. I. Title.
  BV4817.D88 2009
  248.4--dc22
                                            2009008307

Printed in The United States of America
Fifth printing in 2011

CONTENTS

To Lisa

An exeptional wife, mother, and best friend. Thank you for enduring my own idolatry, but most of all for loving me in spite of it.

Foreword

When God tells us not to worship idols, He is not talking only about idols made of stone or wood. An idol is anything other than the true God. And "idol worship" is not just the physical motion of bowing down. It is the whole attitude of mind that puts anything ahead of God in our lives. Understood in that way, all sin is idolatry. If we are ruled by money, it becomes our god, the god Jesus called "mammon" in Matthew 6:24. Paul said, indeed, that greed is idolatry (Colossians 3:5).

So when we find ourselves going against God's Word, it is helpful to ask the question, "What idol am I worshiping?" That is a powerful question, because it exposes the heart. It asks us to inspect our motives. When I am unkind to my wife, for example, it's not a mere slip. It shows that my heart is not right with God, that I love myself more than my wife rather than giving to her the self-giving love that Jesus gave me (Ephesians 5:25–32). My own convenience, my own preferences, my own comfort have become my idol. When we see our sins this way, as God does, we will be quicker to repent of them.

Thinking about idolatry helps us to measure ourselves accurately, to see how far we fall below God's standards. For sin is never a minor thing: cheating a bit on taxes, taking a doughnut without paying, running a red light, spanking my child out of anger rather than love. We so easily dismiss these things as minor and come up feeling that we are doing pretty well in our Christian walk. But God won't let us off that easily. These actions are symptoms of something deep. Sin is always a heart condition. God wants us to note them and grieve for them. We have exchanged God's truth for a lie, His glory for other gods. Only when we recognize this can we see how precious, by contrast, is the true and living God, and His Son Jesus Christ.

And God wants us not just to acknowledge Christ, but to acclaim Him, to praise Him, to recognize Him with our intellect, will, and emotions as the greatest treasure that there is. The greatest treasure deserves the greatest passion, the greatest love.

When we see our sin as idolatry, we come to appreciate far more deeply what Christ has done for us on the cross. Idolatry is a problem we cannot fix, because it goes so deep. It places us under God's wrath and curse, and we can well understand why. Only God's free gift of salvation through Jesus can change our heart and turn it in a new direction.

Greg Dutcher is a man who has thought long and hard about idolatry and has been moved to praise Jesus as his greatest treasure. He is just great at telling stories and providing apt illustrations. He speaks to us where we are and lifts us up to be with Christ. I'm delighted he has published this book, and I pray that it gets a large readership. This book can lead the church out of its complacency with sin and its superficial understanding of redemption. To God be all the glory.

> John M. Frame
> Professor of Systematic Theology
> and Philosophy
> Reformed Theological Seminary

I wanna heal, I wanna feel what I thought was never real.
—Linkin Park

If I find in myself a desire which no experience
in this world can satisfy, the most probable explanation
is that I was made for another world.
—C. S. Lewis

YOU are the
treasure
that I seek . . .

But There's a Lot of Cool Stuff
Out There, Lord

In the jungle underbrush, a young pygmy holds his body as still as the statue he has come to see. A cobra slithers by just a few feet ahead. Had he not spotted and avoided it, the boy's veins would be filling up with venom at this very moment, forever barring him access to the hallowed shrine of the forest spirit. The boy's mother is sick with the fever, and the shaman has guided him to this sacred site to obtain healing. In the remote villages of Cameroon, the holy man's word is gold. To the natural observer, this place is little more than a stick in the ground encircled by smooth gray stones. But the boy believes the shaman's promise; he waits for the snake to pass, then presses onward toward his mother's only hope . . .

After a brief battle with second-guessing, the young female executive takes the $2,700 business suit to the counter and pulls out

her Visa Platinum. She's fairly certain it has a three-thousand-dollar
limit, so she takes a deep breath, tries to look natural, and smiles a
sigh of relief as the handsome cashier—wearing a smile himself, of
course—hands her the receipt to sign.

"My, someone will be looking dynamite tonight, won't she?" he
asks playfully.

The young woman shrugs, as if she's bought several of these
suits before, and casually says, "Nah, just liked the color." The truth
is, she is swimming in debt. Her young husband has begged her to
help work out a realistic budget for the family. Do they have to live
in Midtown? Must they belong to the most expensive health club
in the city when there's a YMCA down the street? But he doesn't
understand what she does; the trappings of success are the proof of
success. With a little luck she'll get one of the VP spots in her firm
within the next year or two. She hopes to. She *has* to . . .

Laying his Bible on the dashboard, the pastor starts the ignition
and pulls out of the church parking lot. "Your sermon was great
today, honey. Did you get any feedback?" asks his wife.

The minister cocks his head slightly, as if retrieving the answer
takes a good deal of effort. After a few moments of "searching"
(after all, people's comments were the furthest thing from his mind),
he responds, "Yes, I think one or two people said they thought it was
helpful. Praise the Lord."

And with that the conversation changes. The pastor looks fully
engaged when his wife talks about the new children's coordinator:
"She's wonderful." But if she could see what's playing out in his mind,
wouldn't she be surprised! The fact is that he received *many* comments about today's sermon: "funny," "inspiring," "solid," "trans-
forming." And every one of those comments is running through

his mind in full Technicolor splendor! He's been in a rut lately, and today he was determined to break free. Looks like he did . . .

Idolatry: It's Not Just for Pygmies Anymore

A pygmy, a young executive, and a preacher—sounds like the start of a bad joke, doesn't it? Could you think of three more distinctly different people from this motley crew? But look more closely: An invisible thread connects them. Each of them is looking for something. In their own way, they are all on a hunt for fulfillment, but none of them is finding it. And that's really the story of the human race, isn't it? Scan through some music stations on your FM dial and listen for the longing. U2 "still hasn't found what they're looking for." Keane's "getting older" and "needs something to rely on." Linkin Park wants to "heal, wants to feel what it thought was never real." We are all longing to arrive on the shores of contentment, to find what will ultimately satisfy us.

The Treasure Hunt

Perhaps this is why Jesus so often used the motifs of quests and treasures in His teaching. A woman loses a valuable coin and rejoices when she finds it. A shepherd goes on an all-out search, leaving the other sheep to secure "the one that got away." And could Jesus be any clearer when He says, "The kingdom of heaven is like treasure hidden in a field, which a man found and covered up. Then in his joy he goes and sells all that he has and buys that field" (Matthew 13:44). The fact that Christ compares receiving Him and His kingdom to discovering a treasure has profound implications for how we understand the Christian faith.

Years ago I talked with a man who told me he was a Buddhist, a Taoist, a Hindu, a Muslim, and a Christian simultaneously. Thinking he was setting me up for one of those "a priest, a rabbi, and a minister all walk into a bar" jokes, I braced myself for a punch line that never came. This man was absolutely serious about his religious identity. When I asked him why he wanted to be an amalgamation of all of these faiths, he simply said, "Doesn't it make sense to have all the bases covered?"

But Jesus' comparison of finding Him to finding a buried treasure won't allow this kind of "play-it-safe" approach. Embracing the Jesus of Scripture is not a roll of the dice or even a reasonable, educated guess. When we receive Christ as Savior we are making a declaration with our very lives that shouts, "I've found it! Jesus is my treasure!" So when somebody becomes a Christian, the quest is over. The story of that person's life has come to a happy ending, right? At the risk of sounding a bit political, we can only say yes—and no.

Conflicted Christians

It is true—there is nothing better than Christ. He is the pearl of great price, and it would be worthwhile for us to sell off every other possession if that's what it required to have Him. He is the answer to the psalmist's question, "Whom have I in heaven but you?" (73:25). The Christian knows that Jesus is not simply the last rest stop before reaching the anticipated destination. Jesus *is* the destination. Even heaven, as wonderful a place as it must be, is merely window dressing when compared to the great inhabitant of heaven. Jesus did not say to the repentant thief on the cross, "Today you will be in Paradise," but rather, "Today you will be *with me* in Paradise" (Luke 23:43, emphasis added). So, we say yes. When we receive Christ as our treasure, we have found the very thing for which our souls have most longed. But the Christian's heart is a funny thing.

We also say no, however, since the treasure hunt is an ongoing process as our hearts keep losing sight of what they know to be supremely valuable. Recall the third example in this chapter's opening, the pastor. He is a man who knows that Christ is the pearl of great price. He invests his life proclaiming that true contentment and satisfaction are found in no one other than Jesus himself. But why does he seem like a vain woman craving compliments on the drive home from church? Doesn't he know better?

Or ask yourself: Do you know better? Let me answer that while you're giving it some thought. After all, I am the pastor in the story. On another Sunday not too long ago, I preached a message where I boldly stated, "Jesus Christ is our everything, or he isn't anything." I meant every word of it. And even when we finished our service by singing that Christ is our strength in weakness, the treasure that we seek, our all in all, I meant every word of that, too.

And then I found myself a few hours later browsing through a catalog of upcoming Macintosh products. It was a calm, casual way to spend a lazy Sunday afternoon. And then—rising like Poseidon out of the glossy-page sea—I saw it: the new iPhone. Wow! A phone, an iPod, and a pocket computer! How could I live another day without one of those? Without realizing it, I lost myself for another hour on the Internet reading any article I could find for more information about this life-changing device. I should have just been honest and prayed, "Lord, you are the treasure that I seek . . . but there's some really cool stuff out there, too." But the disparity between the place Christ *should* hold in our lives and the place He *does* hold should give us hope. It tells us that there is a battle to be fought, a battle that God can fight in and through us.

How Can We Keep Christ at the Center?

I trust that you have picked up this book because, like me, you want your Sunday afternoon experience to line up with those Sunday morning moments when you really do get a glimpse of Jesus as your all-satisfying treasure. My prayer is that this book will help you in this regard, but in order to press forward, we have to take a look at an ugly word, and it's a word that gets little press today. *Idolatry* is an old-fashioned word, consigned to social studies classes and Clive Cussler novels. But what if it's alive and well, even in America? What if it's a problem of such epidemic proportions that our unawareness of it is only making it worse? But more importantly, what if we could isolate this problem, like a disease, and contain it before it destroys us? As you'll see in the chapters ahead, the stakes are very high. The battle against idolatry is a fight for our lives, the lives of others, and, most importantly, the reputation of Christ himself. I invite you to learn more about this syndrome, its pathology and its remedy, and join me, another recovering idolater, on a journey of eternal significance. There is good news to be found in the pages ahead, but we need to start with the bad news first. The remedy, like most, can only be appreciated when we understand the illness for what it is. May the Lord Jesus bless you as you lay your heart open before Him.

Prayer

Lord Jesus, take from us now everything that would hinder the closest communion with God. Any wish or desire that might hamper us in prayer remove, we pray You. Any memory of either sorrow or care that might hinder the fixing of our affection wholly on our God, take it away now. What have we to do with idols any more? You have seen and observed us. You know where the difficulty lies. Help us against it, and may we now come boldly, not in the Holy place alone, but in the Holiest of all, where we should not dare to come if our great Lord had not torn the veil, sprinkled the mercy seat with His own blood, and asked us to enter.

—Charles Spurgeon

Study Guide

1. Can you think of other contemporary songs, films, books, or television shows that capture the universal longing in people's hearts to find ultimate satisfaction in something?

2. Glance through the many parables Jesus tells in Matthew 13. Where else do you see the theme of treasure, joy, and ultimate satisfaction described? In what ways are they similar to the little parable in verse 44? In what ways are they different?

3. If you wanted to tell a twenty-first-century version of one of these parables, what story would you tell?

4. Can you relate to showing more interest in a nifty gadget than in Christ? In what way?

The more one analyzes people, the more all reasons for analysis disappear. Sooner or later one comes to that dreadful universal thing called human nature.

—Oscar Wilde

Man is wrong at the center of his being, and therefore everything is wrong.

—Martyn Lloyd-Jones

See, this alone I found, that God made man upright, but they have sought out many schemes.

—Ecclesiastes 7:29

"I'VE got some bad news for YOU . . ."

The Nightmare

"I'm afraid I've got some bad news for you . . ."

Is there anywhere to go but down from an introduction like that? Pick any scenario:

- Your lawyer tells you the best you will get is five to ten years.
- Your mechanic describes a shot transmission, when you thought it just needed a tune-up.
- Your son's teacher informs you that young Jeremy will have to repeat the fourth grade next year.
- Your loan officer notifies you that you have been denied.

The list could go on and on. If someone starts a sentence with these words, you brace yourself for what's coming. But look at the examples again. One is glaringly absent, isn't it? We would take any of the above scenarios over the one we all fear the most.

• Your doctor enters the small, sterile exam room. His expression is grim, and suddenly your heart starts working overtime. Without comment he places your chart on the table. He turns to you and says, *"I'm afraid I have some bad news for you . . ."*

Many of you reading this book have not experienced this checkup-turned-nightmare, but you probably know someone who has. Most of us are able to muster up enough compassion for those "less fortunate" people to say, "Man, that's terrible." Few of us are honest enough, however, to say what we're really thinking: "I'm so glad it's not me."

The Tenuous Comfort of Statistics

It seems that what enables us to live each day in a world where tragedy strikes all around us is the probability that it will not strike us directly. We roll the dice and rest reasonably assured that the odds are in our favor. Those poor souls whose doctors approach them with a dreaded diagnosis are, hopefully, "other people." The statistics are on most people's sides, though, right?

But what if there is a bullet that you cannot dodge? What if there is a deadly virus with your name on it? What if you looked around and saw that no one, including you, was lucky enough to be on vacation when this germ spread and got the whole neighborhood quarantined?

By now you may be looking at the cover to make sure you didn't inadvertently pick up the latest Stephen King novel. The sad truth, however, is that you have *already* been diagnosed with something worse than anything horror fiction can depict. God himself, in the person of His Son, Jesus Christ, the Great Physician, has entered the exam room of history with a diagnosis most people simply dismiss. Tragically, they consider this doctor a "quack" and go about their lives not knowing that something is rapidly eating them from the inside out.

A Divine Diagnosis

Where do we find such a sobering analysis? Quite frankly, there are countless such descriptions from Genesis through Revelation. Yet one of the most concise diagnoses is found in Paul's letter to the church at Rome.

After a brief introduction of himself and his travel plans, Paul tells the young church at Rome why the gospel is such a precious thing. To do so, he chooses the conventional way of giving the bad news first.

When my brother-in-law was a teenager, he had an interesting way of lessening the impact of his father's discipline. If he came home in violation of his curfew, he would say, "Dad, I'm really sorry, but I wrecked the car." When Dad's eyes swelled with horror, David would smile and say, "Just kidding, Dad." I do not remember my brother-in-law ever evading punishment with this tactic, but to this day he insists it helped dampen the fires of his father's wrath. He was convinced that the temporary image of a wrecked Toyota would sweeten the lesser crime of a broken curfew.

Paul, on the other hand, does not fabricate stories to make the gospel look any better; he does not have to. He needs only to tell the truth: Humanity is a wreck, headed for the scrap heap. Notice how Paul minces no words when he makes his candid observations.

For the wrath of God is revealed from heaven against *all ungodliness and unrighteousness of men*, who by their unrighteousness suppress the truth. For what can be known about God is plain to them, because God has shown it to them. For his invisible attributes, namely, his eternal power and divine nature, have been clearly perceived, ever since the creation of the world, in the things that have been made. So they are without excuse. For although they knew God, they did not honor him as God or give thanks to him, but they *became futile in their thinking*, and their *foolish hearts were darkened*. Claiming to be wise, *they became fools . . .* (Romans 1:18–22, emphasis added).

Paul is not describing a segment of the human race.[1] His task here is much more daunting than commenting on a particular group of people living in a particular time and place. The context of the book of Romans makes it clear that he is describing Jew and Gentile (a Hebrew way of dividing up the whole world into two groups). Paul's role is that of a physician's assistant. He enters the exam room with divine X-rays and tells it like it is. God's flawless diagnosis of the human race is not pretty. We would love to hear words like *good, honorable, compassionate, wise*. Instead, we wince at the words used to describe our present condition: *ungodliness, unrighteousness, futile thinking, foolish hearts, fools.*

There is no dodging the divine analysis of the human heart; it is diseased. We are plagued by an eternally terminable illness. We may work hard, play hard, get married, make love, eat voraciously, laugh loudly, and dance the night away. But God knows that underneath the veneer of such carefree lives, we are decomposing.

Cynthia was one of the most vivacious, joyful Christians I have ever known. If I ever wanted to shake off the Sunday morning sloth that so often made my worship of God drudgery, I needed only to watch Cynthia worship. She was absolutely captivating. Her joyful

---

1. Many have pointed out that in this particular section, Paul appears to indict only the ancient Gentile world for its pagan idolatry, but if you follow Paul's argument through the first three chapters of Romans, you see "that all, both Jews and Greeks, are under sin" (Romans 3:9).

response to the songs, prayers, and sermon (even the announcements) put me to shame. Her intense energy was all I needed to pray, "Lord, let me worship you like that!" Then one day she waited in that small, sterile exam room. The doctor entered with a grim expression and . . . well, you can imagine the rest.

I could barely believe it when I sat by her bedside in the hospice facility a few days before she died. The cancer had overrun her body. Her once vibrant face had been drained of all its color. She struggled with all of her fading strength to take each breath. As I silently wept and prayed for this woman I loved, I strove to convince myself that this was still Cynthia. Perhaps the most disturbing thought was that her disease had been working around the clock to kill her years earlier when she was at her liveliest.

What is true of the human body proves true of the human spirit as well. Despite a healthy outward appearance, our hearts are slowly dying as a spiritual sickness works to bring about our demise.

A Frightening Prognosis

We are accustomed to even the worst of human illnesses coming to a merciful end. When Cynthia died, virtually everyone who came to visit the family said something like, "She's not suffering any more." As a pastor, I found myself comforting the family with some of the same sentiments. For all of its terrors, even the most dreadful disease has to stop eventually. Tragically, the spiritual virus Paul describes has no such happy ending.

Paul says that this disease never reaches a peak from where it mercifully descends (like it does for the cancer patient at death). This kind of illness gets worse and worse, with no relief in sight. In fact, it leads to God's eternal wrath (Romans 1:18; 2:5), which lands us on an everlasting deathbed, separated from God himself. Surely we can understand why so many people might be inclined to dismiss Paul as a loon. We want doctors to give us good news, and if they cannot do that, we at least want them to sugarcoat the bad news! But no amount of "wordsmithing" can change the facts. The late A. W. Tozer said it well:

> God's justice stands forever against the sinner in utter severity. The vague and tenuous hope that God is too kind to punish the ungodly has become a deadly opiate for the consciences of millions. It hushes their fears and allows them to practice all pleasant forms of iniquity while death draws every day nearer and the command to repent goes unregarded. As responsible moral beings we dare not so trifle with our eternal future.[2]

Tozer's words put us in a place of crisis: God's diagnosis—or our wishful thinking. If we are duped into thinking that the human condition is not diseased or that if it is, it is infected with only the mildest of viruses, then we are doomed. The only way to be convinced that this malady is deadly is to put it under a microscope and carefully study its pathology. Just what is this hideous thing that has infected the human race?

Prayer

Search me, O God, and know my heart!
Try me and know my thoughts!
And see if there be any grievous way in me,
and lead me in the way everlasting!

Psalm 139:23–24

---

2. *The Knowledge of the Holy.* New York: Harper Collins, 1978.

Study Guide

1. Have you or someone you love ever experienced the "bad news in the doctor's office" scenario? How did it change your (or your loved one's) perspective on life?

2. Why do you think it is so difficult for people to accept that they are spiritually diseased, that their eternal souls are in danger? How would it change people's perspectives if they acknowledged their true condition?

3. Read Romans 1:28–32. In this list of sins, do you see yourself? What do you think of the fact that "gossips," "disobedience to parents," and "envy" are listed alongside of "haters of God" and "murder"?

4. Some contemporary church leaders have suggested that unbelievers should not be exposed to concepts like sin, judgment, and wrath in a worship service since they might be "turned off." How do you feel about this suggestion in light of what has been discussed in this chapter?

I'll make him an offer he can't refuse.
—from *The Godfather*

The created universe is all about glory. The deepest
longing of the human heart and the deepest meaning of heaven
and earth are summed up in this: the glory of God . . .
The universe was made to show it, and we were made to see it
and savor it. Which is why the world is as disordered
and as dysfunctional as it is. We have exchanged
the glory of God for other things.
—John Piper

Now the serpent was more crafty than any other beast of the field
that the Lord God had made. He said to the woman, "Did God
actually say, 'You shall not eat of any tree in the garden'?"
—Genesis 3:1

the ESSENCE of
idolatry

What's in a Name?

No, the term *idolatry syndrome* cannot be found in Scripture, so it may seem that I am starting this journey on the wrong foot. My hope, however, is that the expression will prove helpful in ways that other non-biblical phrases have benefited Christians in the past. *Quiet times, devotions,* and *small groups* are not terms that can be found in the Bible, but they certainly do have biblical content. I pray that my use of the phrase in this book will adequately reflect the Bible's teaching on the tragedy of the human condition.

In the same chapter where Paul gives the diagnosis of humanity's illness, we get a glimpse of the nature of the disease that plagues us. Let's pick up where we left off.

Claiming to be wise, they became fools, and *exchanged* the glory of the immortal God for images resembling mortal man and birds and animals and reptiles. Therefore God gave them up in the lusts of their hearts to impurity, to the dishonoring of their bodies among themselves, because they *exchanged* the truth about God for a lie and worshiped and served the creature rather than the Creator, who is blessed forever! Amen (Romans 1:22–25, emphasis added).

I took a college philosophy class my freshman year. The professor was a no-nonsense kind of instructor. When describing the four papers we would be required to write that semester, a student, aiming for a moment of levity, raised his hand and asked, "Can I just write one paper on what went wrong with the human race?" A few students chuckled at the second-rate joke, but the professor simply replied, "One paper won't do it, young friend. You're already about ten thousand pages behind even the most mediocre thinker on that subject."

How ironic that Paul condenses the tens of thousands of pages written on what went wrong with the human race into three verses! With the precision of a scientist, the apostle isolates the origin of mankind's fall from grace in just one word: *exchanged*.

A Bum Tradeoff

In many ways, our entire lives are about exchanging things. Every day we attempt to get the better end of the deal. That Starbucks coffee we buy every morning does more for us than the cash in our pockets. The cup of java is a prize, so we happily part with a couple of dollars to get it. That morning run seems like pure torture when we're all wrapped up in our warm blankets. The fifteen minutes of extra sleep hold more attraction than the negligible benefits of a single jog, so we gladly hit the snooze button to go back to our dreaming.

From time to time though, we get burned. The coffee is stale. We'd have been better off to make a cup at home. We feel sluggish at work. It would have been better to put on our Nikes and hit the streets. We kick ourselves when we get a bum tradeoff.

Careful readers of Paul's words should slam their palms to their foreheads in regret. They see that the apostle boils all of humanity's problems down to a bad trade. In verse 22 we learn that mankind swapped the masterpiece of God for a garage sale counterfeit. Man had the beauty and majesty of the God of the universe right before his eyes, and he decided he didn't like the view. We turned our back on God, looked at the world around us (forgetting who made it in the first place), and said, "Now, this is where the action is. Men, women, money, things—these are worth living for."

Pastor John Piper effectively captures this principle when he asserts, "That is the fundamental problem with the human race. We do not acknowledge, value, treasure, savor, honor, or make much of the greatest value in the universe, the glory of God. That is our wickedness and our disease and our great mutiny against God."[3]

Paul then says that we not only exchanged God's glory for our vainglory, but we also traded eternal truth for a pack of lies, "[We] exchanged the truth about God for a lie." Even though we could have seen life through crystal clear lenses, we chose the "rose-colored" lenses of our fevered imagination. It is interesting that Paul simply calls what we traded in for truth "a lie." It is an all-inclusive term that boldly declares the hollowness of anything or anyone other than God. Paul does not need to recite the menu of other options the world offers us. Humanism, atheism, polytheism, hedonism, nor any other "ism" needs to be carefully examined to see if it stands as an equally viable alternative to the truth of God. All rival worldviews fall under the category of "a lie" when compared to the God of Scripture. This is why the most diverse kinds of worshipers can be lumped together. The naturalist worships the earth. The humanist worships man. The atheist worships nothing. Each has

---

3. "The First Dark Exchange," http://www.desiringgod.org/ResourceLibrary/Sermons/ByDate/1998/1052_The_First_Dark_Exchange_Idolatry/

traded in the truth of God for a bogus belief system. Each person, then, worships "a lie."

Is It Really That Simple?

Can you imagine the time and money we could save if our society accepted this assessment of the human predicament? Think about the number of committees, programs, and congressional initiatives that have been formed to investigate, assess, and resolve mankind's various maladies. Alcoholism, crime, drugs, racism, teenage pregnancy, terrorism, and a host of other ills plague our world. For each atrocity, scores of taskforces are established to tackle the problem. But Paul comes to us with a simple analysis: The problem is that man exchanged God for a cheap substitute, and look where it's gotten us!

Humanity's illness is the idolatry syndrome. We were infected when our first parents considered a piece of fruit sweeter than fellowship with God. We were ruined when they deemed the word of a snake better than the promise of "a God who cannot lie" (Titus 1:2). They compared. They calculated. They traded in God for a "better model." We've been doomed ever since.

Interestingly, we might think that when Eden was off limits, when work made us sweat, and when God was hidden from our sight, that we would have fallen to our knees and begged for mercy. But that's not how the idolatry syndrome works. Once our souls are contaminated, the desire for more substitutes only grows.

Meal-Replacement Drinks Are Great for the First Five Minutes

The biblical writers mention no world conferences where mankind convenes to discuss how we all might return to the God we've rejected. Rather, we read of substitution after substitution, as God is continually traded for idols. The writer of Ecclesiastes serves as a representative for the human race when he recounts his wasted life. He experimented with architecture, philosophy, food, wine, women, and song (chapters 1 and 2). Yet near the end of his life, he assesses how he has spent his years. "Then I considered all that my hands had done and the toil I had expended in doing it, and behold, all was *vanity* and a *striving after wind* and there was *nothing to be gained* under the sun" (Ecclesiastes 2:11, emphasis added).

Those infected with the idolatry syndrome have no hope of finding the life God originally intended for them. An existence spent exchanging God for counterfeits is destined for disaster, both in this life and the next. Those suffering from the syndrome never realize that the reason they feel so purposeless is that an idol cannot satisfy a heart designed to experience God.

Every now and then I convince myself that I can actually do one of those diets where you drink two meal-replacement shakes a day. It always starts off pretty well, as I convince myself that a powdery, eight-ounce drink has done the trick. *It was just as good as a sausage and cheese omelet*, I tell myself. My resistance usually breaks down somewhere around 10:30 a.m. As my hunger intensifies, I can't even comfort myself with the promise of a turkey club at noon—just another shake to hold me until my "sensible" dinner. Why am I so miserable on such a weight-loss plan? Because a can of artificially sweetened "milk" is a lousy substitute for a good meal.

Is There Any Hope?

An idol is a lousy substitute for God. And as long as people refuse to return to the Creator, they move from one substitute to another, searching in vain for the satisfaction of their own souls. The early church father Augustine once prayed, "You have formed us for yourself and our hearts are restless until they find rest in you." Sadly, it seems that many people will never enter into this kind of peace. Jesus said, "Enter by the narrow gate. For the gate is wide and the way is easy that leads to destruction, and those who enter by it are many" (Matthew 7:13).

Yet is there a way to find rest for our restless hearts? Is the idolatry syndrome an incurable disease? Are people who have put their trust in Christ still infected? Can we actually find a lifelong remedy that will free us from the ravaging effects of this virus?

To these and many other questions we now turn. May the Great Physician himself help us understand what is killing us, and, more importantly, how to kill it back!

Prayer

Eternal God, in whom we live and move and have our being, whose face is hidden from us by our sins, and whose mercy we forget in the blindness of our hearts: cleanse us from all our offenses, and deliver us from proud thoughts and vain desires, that with reverent and humble hearts we may draw near to you, confessing our faults, confiding in your grace, and finding in you our refuge and strength; through Jesus Christ your Son.

—Book of Common Worship

Study Guide

1. Read Romans 1:22. If the essence of idolatry is exchanging God for something else, then what are some fresher ways to describe particular sins? What is the good that we give up, and what is the alleged "prize" that we receive? Note the first example and fill in the list below.

The Sin	What's Given Up	What's "Gained"
Cheating on taxes	God-glorifying honesty and stewardship	Money
Adultery		
Gossip		
Gluttony		

2. Read Psalm 115. How are idols contrasted with God? How should we feel when we read this psalm and reflect upon the nature of our idols?

3. The writer of Ecclesiastes is a vivid example of someone who demonstrates the tragedy of a life devoted to worthless substitutes for God. Can you think of any modern examples of the same type of person?

4. Take some time for some prayerful introspection. Do you see areas of your life that reveal a greater hunger for substitutes than for God himself?

We believe that the history of the world is but
the history of His influence and that the center of
the whole universe is the cross of Calvary.
—Alexander MacLaren

The cross is the lightning rod of grace that
short-circuits God's wrath to Christ so that only
the light of His love remains for sinners.
—A. W. Tozer

For I decided to know nothing among you except
Jesus Christ and him crucified.
—the apostle Paul, 1 Corinthians 2:2

the cross
of CHRIST
safety
in the ashes

Boasting in What?

Imagine yourself sitting in the posh Kodak Theater for this year's Academy Awards ceremony. A famous director is called to the stage to receive a coveted honorary achievement award. As he runs through a list of names you've never heard, you find yourself drifting off in a daydream, hoping the Best Actor or Best Picture Oscar is coming up soon. Just as you're really starting to check out, the director says something that shocks you back to attention.

". . . and I have something in my pocket that I've never showed another living soul. It's the most important thing in my life. Without it, I would not be who I am."

Now your interest in the director has dramatically increased, and you can barely contain your suspense. *Come on, come on*, you think. *What is it in your pocket?* You're guessing it's a picture of someone—his wife, his child, a good friend perhaps. Or maybe it's just a memento from such a person. While you're guessing, he finally reaches into his lapel and pulls out a . . . *What! Is that what I think it is?* You think you know, but how could that possibly be?

"This is a potassium chloride syringe. It is used to inject liquid death into the veins of a condemned criminal. It's the greatest thing in my life," says the director.

It's hard to think of something more bizarre, isn't it? But whatever confusion you may be feeling right now is probably very similar to the bewilderment the Christians at Galatia experienced when Paul wrote, "But far be it from me to boast except in the cross of our Lord Jesus Christ" (Galatians 6:14). The cross was the first-century equivalent of the potassium chloride syringe, the electric chair, the noose, or the gas chamber. What was it about such a barbaric instrument of death that made it Paul's only ground of boasting? The answer is, quite frankly, a matter of life or death. For all of us have been infected with this deadly virus called the idolatry syndrome. The cross is its only antidote.

Christ's Decisive Moment

Jesus Christ came into this world to rescue idolaters. The problem was that idolaters were not interested in Christ, the very embodiment of the thing they traded in: the glory of God. How ironic that humans were given another opportunity to behold the glory of God in Christ—"And the Word became flesh and dwelt among us, and we have seen his glory, glory as of the only Son from the Father" (John 1:14)—and they still refused to receive this glory as their greatest treasure. Instead we continued to cling to our counterfeits and substitutes.

Jesus did not shrink back, however, from His mission to rescue us. In fact, He humbly chose to share His life with twelve men who would by and large abandon Him in His hour of need. But just before His idolatrous clan hit the road, we find them together (well, sort of together) on a mount called Olives. The disciples are with Jesus only in terms of their close proximity. Their hearts are far from cherishing His presence among them; in fact, they've all drifted off to sleep. Let's behold the Savior as He anguishes there before His Father.

And there appeared to him an angel from heaven, strengthening him. And being in an agony he prayed more earnestly; and his sweat became like great drops of blood falling down to the ground.

Luke 22:43–44

The only other time an angel appeared to strengthen Jesus was just after his forty-day fast, which culminated in a bout with the devil himself (Matthew 4:1–11). There we see the Savior in a state of such physical weakness that He was probably barely able to stand up, which was why angels came to minister to Him. So this passage in Gethsemane begs the question: Just what is happening here that requires an angel to come to strengthen Jesus? Notice that Jesus is sweating drops of blood to the ground after the angel's appearance. What is it that Jesus is wrestling with here that causes Him such agony—even after receiving supernatural assistance? Many different answers have been suggested.

Some have proposed that Jesus is overwhelmed with the physical pain He is about to experience. And who can doubt the severity of that anguish? In the next twenty hours or so, He will go without sleep, be on trial six times, be scourged, mocked, punched, spit upon, and deprived of all physical comforts. But ensuing physical challenges are not what He is wrestling with on the Mount of Olives.

Others have suggested that Jesus is dealing with the emotional pain He will soon bear. Again, it's hard to argue with this in light of Judas' betrayal, Peter's cowardice, and the fickle crowd's rejection of Him as Messiah. But this is not what He is wrestling with in Gethsemane either.

The careful reader will notice that Jesus tells us precisely what He is wrestling with. But to understand His anguish, let's back up and consider something Jesus knew all too well: the Old Testament.

The Ominous Cup

The Old Testament Jew was well acquainted with a number of metaphors for God's wrath. Darkness, thunder, the winepress— such images pictorially captured the severity of God's hatred of sin. But there was another symbol that Israel was quite familiar with. The following passages depict it graphically.

> *But it is God who executes judgment, putting down one and lifting up another. For in the hand of the Lord there is a* cup *with foaming wine, well mixed, and he pours out from it, and all the wicked of the earth shall drain it down to the dregs* (emphasis added).
>
> Psalm 75:7–8

> *Wake yourself, wake yourself, stand up, O Jerusalem, you who have drunk from the hand of the Lord the* cup *of his wrath, who have drunk to the dregs the bowl, the* cup *of staggering* (emphasis added).
>
> Isaiah 51:17

The cup was a dreadful symbol of the deserved wrath of God. When the Almighty visited a city with His cup of wrath, His enemies had to drink it down to the dregs. But never had the total measure of God's wrath, the eternal weight of it, been poured out before. Yes, there were "previews" of that wrath throughout the Old Testament when places like Sodom and Gomorrah were destroyed. Yet the full fury of that wrath was not poured out until . . . Let's go back to the Mount of Olives and see what Christ is wrestling with.

The Horrible Abyss Jesus Faced . . . for Us!

Jesus is on the ground, sweating drops of blood, because He is wrestling with the cup of His Father's wrath. "Father, if you are willing, remove this *cup* from me," Christ asks (Luke 22:42, emphasis added). What Jesus struggled with there was unspeakable: the full measure of the Father's wrath, the punishment that should have been poured out on those who deemed God less worthy than idols. But Christ emerges from His time of prayer, prepares to be arrested, and sets His face like flint to enter the hell waiting for Him.

And here I would like to address my fellow idolaters. What are we to make of this? Could we possibly be so deeply loved by the Savior that He was willing to swallow hell itself for us? Is it true that when Jesus cried out, "My God, my God, why have you forsaken me?" on the cross, that He was actually experiencing the forsakenness and wrath we deserve? R. C. Sproul provocatively describes Christ's scream as "the scream of the damned. For us."[4] This is the kind of love the Savior has for us who cling to cheap counterfeits and substitutes. Theologian Richard Allen Bodey writes, "He drank the cup bone dry, leaving not a drop for us to drink."[5]

Safety in the Ashes

There is a story of a father and son who are walking across rolling fields of dry grass during the brushfire season. As they look off

---

4. *Tabletalk*, May 1999.
5. *The Voice from the Cross*. Grand Rapids, Michigan: Kregel Publications, 1990.

in the distance, their worst fears are realized. A wall of fire is steadily moving toward them, carried on the wind. They try to run with all their might, only to realize that the fire is faster then they are. Coming to a stop, the boy buries his face in his father's side, awaiting his doom. Just before the fire reaches them, the father surprises his son by reaching into his pocket and pulling out a book of matches. He strikes a match and proceeds to light the entire book on fire; then he tosses the mini inferno behind them. In the fierce wind a new wall of fire has risen behind them. So now a fire blazes behind them, and one rushes toward them. At the last second the father scoops up the son and gently steps backwards, into the charred ashes of the fire he has just lit. When the oncoming wall of fire reaches their spot, it has nothing to fuel itself with in the charred remains of the other fire. They are safe.

The point? If you want to be safe from a fire, you must go to the place where fire has already burned. In Scripture there is only one place where a sinner can find safety from the wrath of God: the cross, a place where God's wrath has already burned. It was there that Jesus took our place and drank the cup of wrath all idolaters deserve.

This book is focused mainly on what *we* have exchanged, the glory of God for idols. But for a moment, let's focus on what *Jesus* has exchanged for us. In order to rescue us from our sin and idolatry, Jesus exchanged His perfect righteousness for our sin and condemnation. This is what Paul meant when he said, "[God] made him to be sin who knew no sin, so that in him we might become the righteousness of God (2 Corinthians 5:21). At the cross, Jesus takes our sin and idolatry and gives us His perfect standing with the Father so that we are forever beyond the reach of condemnation. The cross is literally the reversal of the idolatry syndrome. As one anonymous author put it, "Christ became the very thing that He hated so that we could become the very thing that He loved."

What This Book Is Not

This book is not a self-help manual that will enable you to escape God's wrath. Only the cross of Christ can free us from such a fate. If you have never given your life to Christ who has borne your wrath, then I urge you to put this book down and cry out to the Savior for the mercy you so desperately need. He promises to give it to you.

If you have embraced Jesus as your wrath-bearing Savior, and, like me, you're discouraged that you still find your heart cherishing other things more than Christ, then read on. I write mainly for you. While idolatry cannot eternally condemn us any more, it can rob us of the joy that we could have when Christ is our heart's greatest treasure. It can subtly surface when we least expect it and sidetrack us in our love and devotion to Him. We who have been forever freed from idolatry's penalty can devote the rest of our lives seeking to cherish Christ more than anything else. We do this not to earn anything (How could we?) but to express everything—that Jesus is worthy of all our affection and devotion. After basking in what Jesus has done for us, let's pursue Him with all of our hearts, ready to tear down any idols that block our view of His beauty!

Prayer

Lord Jesus, you are my righteousness, I am your sin. You took on you what was mine; yet set on me what was yours. You became what you were not, that I might become what I was not.

—Martin Luther

Study Guide

1. The symbol of the cross has become so familiar to people today that it is rarely thought of as a barbaric instrument of torture and execution. Besides the potassium chloride syringe, what are some other ways we can capture the nature of the cross to relate to a contemporary audience?

2. In light of what Jesus truly experienced on the cross, how would you seek to explain the significance of Christ's cry, "My God, my God, why have you forsaken me?" (Matthew 27:46) to an unbeliever?

3. How could dwelling on what Jesus did for us on the cross make us more sensitive to idolatry in our lives?

I don't know who my neighbors are.
And there's bars on the corners and bars on my heart.
—Tim McGraw, "Where the Green Grass Grows"

The heart wants what it wants.
—Woody Allen

Archeology limits idols to stone statues; biblical theology
teaches that idols are anything that takes the place of God
in our lives. When understood this way, we can realize that
idolatry is not ancient history but is alive and flourishing
in America as we rush toward the twenty-first century.
—Tom Steller, 1985 sermon

5

INDIANA JONES and the theology of doom

Movies Messed Me Up!

Harrison Ford as Indiana Jones was a good hero for me at age eleven. It was 1981, and I had to wait for two long years to see the conclusion to the first *Star Wars* trilogy. In that sci-fi epic, Ford's character, Han Solo, was frozen in Darth Vader's ice chamber, and young movie fans all over the world lived a tortured existence, not knowing Solo's fate until 1983. Fortunately, *Raiders of the Lost Ark* served as a temporary distraction. In this movie Harrison Ford emerged in the role of an archeologist/superhero. Is there anyone who has seen this movie who doesn't remember the famous scene where Indiana outruns a rolling boulder? Indiana's adventures entertained me well. Sadly, they also warped my view of reality.

Most of us have an "Indiana Jones" view of idolatry. We hear the word *idols* and think about jungle tribes and totem poles. Idolatry is something that happens "out there" in obscure parts of the world most of us will see only on the Discovery Channel. Modern

Americans have more sophisticated problems like stress, financial pressure, and job dissatisfaction; idolatry doesn't even make the top twenty. Our theology of idolatry is, as one scholar I know put it, "totally messed up." Let's see if we can get our thinking back on track.

An Affair of the Heart

We can learn a lot about human nature by reading about the ancient nation of Israel. The Israelites were infatuated with God substitutes. Granted, in the Old Testament, most of the idols described were material in nature. People worshiped graven images, statues— even the sun, moon, and stars. A cursory glance at Israel's history could lead us to think that all Israel needed to do to avoid idolatry was to steer clear of certain geographical places, "temple of doom" places. Enter God's prophets, however, and such an understanding of idolatry evaporates.

God's prophets played a critical role in Israel's history. They were charged with the awesome responsibility of proclaiming God's perspective on the ever-changing national scene. R. C. Sproul writes, "In Israel the prophets served as God's prosecuting attorneys. Armed with divine subpoenas, they were to file suit against Israel for breaking their covenant with God."[6] Ezekiel was such a prophet.

Whisked away by an enemy nation, Ezekiel found himself stuck with the difficult task of comforting his fellow captives in the pagan land of Babylon, a cesspool of idolatry. The Jews wept when they surveyed the landscape and saw no temple for Yahweh, the God of Israel. The pathos of their misery is captured in the opening words of Psalm 137:1–4.

---

6. *The Soul's Quest for God*. Wheaton, Illinois: Tyndale, 1992.

By the waters of Babylon
   there we sat down and wept,
   when we remembered Zion.
On the willows there
   we hung up our lyres.
For there our captors
   required of us songs,
and our tormentors, mirth, saying,
   "Sing us one of the songs of Zion!"
How shall we sing the Lord's song in a foreign land?

Babylon was a wicked place, chockfull of altars, statues, and temples to false gods. The natural question any Israelite would ask a spokesman for God was, "Why? What have we done to deserve such humiliation at the hands of these barbarians?" In Ezekiel 14:1–6, the prophet describes such a scene.

Then certain of the elders of Israel came to me and sat before me. And the word of the Lord came to me: "Son of man, these men have taken their idols into their hearts, and set the stumbling block of their iniquity before their faces. Should I indeed let myself be consulted by them? Therefore speak to them and say to them, Thus says the Lord God: Any one of the house of Israel who takes his idols into his heart and sets the stumbling block of his iniquity before his face, and yet comes to the prophet, I the Lord will answer him as he comes with the multitude of his idols, that I may lay hold of the hearts of the house of Israel, who are all estranged from me through their idols.

"Therefore say to the house of Israel, Thus says the Lord God: Repent and turn away from your idols, and turn away your faces from all your abominations."

The elders of Israel were the religious elite, not unlike the professional clergy of today. The average Israelite would have looked to them for guidance in a dark time. But things were so dark in Babylon that even the pros didn't have the answers. The fact that the elders came and sat down in front of Ezekiel shows their deference to the prophet. Maybe God had revealed some kind of rhyme or reason to an amateur. It seemed worth a shot to ask him, "Why, Ezekiel? What has caused this mess?" Ezekiel's answer is straightforward: idolatry.

Idolatry? Wasn't that a Babylonian problem? The elders of Israel would have been the first to rise up in protest at the detestable altars and shrines that filled this wicked, foreign land. With religious zeal they would have denounced the religion of Babylon as a vile, idolatrous faith. Ezekiel's identification of idolatry as the heart of Israel's problem is similar to telling a diehard Redskin's fan that his problem is that he loves the Dallas Cowboys too much! (If you ever do this, duck—fast!) So was Ezekiel blind, stupid, insane? Couldn't he see that the religious pros had nothing to do with idols?

Yet the prophet's observation was not based on surveying hillsides, but hearts. "These men have set up idols in their hearts," he says. Think about that statement. We don't need to travel to distant jungles to find a place where idolatry is practiced; idolatry is going on *inside* of us. Hundreds of years later, Paul would diagnose what Ezekiel observes here. The diagnosis is crystal clear; the people are infected with the idolatry syndrome. Their hearts have made the dark exchange. God has been traded in for a better model.

Ezekiel doesn't let us in on the type of idols the Israelites had erected in their hearts. Was it pride, lust, the fear of man? We don't know. The prophet is more concerned about the root of their idolatry than the fruit. The pathetic substitutes for God were not being manufactured in a Babylonian assembly line; they were being generated in a far darker place—the infected hearts of a sinful people. But let's leave Israel in Babylon for the time being and come back to America.

America, the Beautiful?

As I write I'm enjoying the warmth of a thoroughly suburban kitchen. A pot of decaf is brewing just within my reach, my wife is enjoying a rerun of *ER*, and my six-year-old-son is sleeping peacefully under his Spiderman comforter upstairs. How quaint! How American! Isn't this kind of scene typical of homes all across this country? It seems to me that we are a long way from Babylon.

The prophet's words haunt me, however. I cannot comfort myself by consigning idolatry to distant times and places. What is my son dreaming of right now? Do sweet dreams of bigger and better toys call to him in his slumber? As she watches Dr. Carter resuscitate a drowning victim, is my wife harboring (maybe enjoying!) a grudge against me over unkind words I've recently said to her? And what about me? Why am I preaching sermons every Sunday? Is it really for God's glory—or at least for the benefit of the sheep? Or am I secretly hoping for the grand-slam sermon that keeps the compliments coming? The fact that Ezekiel traces idolatry's origin to our hearts, instead of shrines, forces me to ask such questions—even here in my comfortable, American kitchen!

But there's another problem here in the suburbs, isn't there? None of my neighbors bow to the same idol; after all, each person's heart is busy manufacturing its own god. We live in the age of customized upgrades and "have it your way" menu options. Unlike Israel, we do not have a tabernacle or temple, a common meeting place to worship the same God. The closest we get is the mall parking lot—but once we walk through the doors, we make a beeline for our favorite store. The point is, idolatry cuts us off from one another. All of us are locked into personalized prisons of our own making. Is it any wonder that we'd rather chat online with a total stranger than have a day-to-day relationship with our next-door neighbors? Idolatry kills community.

I wonder how things might radically change in our churches if we became convinced that idolatry was our greatest problem. What if angry husbands stopped blaming their wives for their own unhappiness and just took a good hard look into their own hearts? What would they find—perhaps that their own idols were in conflict with those of their wives? What if "model" parents actually acknowledged that their firm discipline was little more than a program to produce quiet kids who impress their friends across the aisle? What if the church stopped trying to help its members with pop psychology and told them that their real problem is idol worship?

Let's commit ourselves now to mastering the pathology of idolatry. Let's turn that ridiculous old cliché upside down to say what it really should: "What we *don't* know *can* hurt us."

Prayer

Behold, I was brought forth in iniquity,
and in sin did my mother conceive me.
Behold, you delight in truth in the inward being,
and you teach me wisdom in the secret heart.
Purge me with hyssop, and I shall be clean;
wash me, and I shall be whiter than snow.
Let me hear joy and gladness;
let the bones that you have broken rejoice.

Hide your face from my sins,
*   and blot out all my iniquities.*
Create in me a clean heart, O God,
*   and renew a right spirit within me.*

Psalm 51:5–10

Study Guide

1. Describe a stereotypical example of an "Indiana Jones" kind of idol? Why do you think it can be dangerous to think of idols in such physical/external ways?

2. Read Ezekiel 14:1–6. The elders of Israel would have been appalled by the shrines and altars that covered the Babylonian landscape. How do you think they felt when Ezekiel told them their idols were within? How do you feel about your own heart's ability to manufacture idols?

3. Since idolatry is born in the hidden place of the heart, it can be "covered up" by things that look downright holy, for example, the preacher craving his listeners' praise for a good sermon. What idolatrous desire could be lurking behind a prayer for healing, an act of charity, an evangelistic encounter, a parent's act of discipline?

4. Give some examples of how chasing after our own idols cuts us off from one another?

It is stupidity rather than courage to refuse to recognize
danger when it is close upon you.
—Sherlock Holmes

Most of God's people are content to be saved from the hell
that is without; they are not so anxious to be saved
from the hell that is within.
—Robert Murray M'Cheyne

And if you do not do well, sin is crouching at the door.
Its desire is for you, but you must rule over it.
—Genesis 4:7

the
stealthy
HUNTER

Anybody Got a Silver Bullet?

Werewolves are outside of our house, savagely scratching at the doors and windows. My older brother Andy and I hastily barricade ourselves in our bedroom. Two young kids can survive this terror only by sticking together. The one thing that gives me comfort is that Andy is with me. At this moment he's no longer my annoying older brother, bullying me, teasing me; he's now my hero. We frantically work to insulate ourselves in our room, when the sounds of the werewolves suddenly cease. My heart is pounding like a jackhammer, but I'm beginning to feel some relief. I turn to Andy, hoping that he too thinks we're safe when . . . Have you guessed it? Yeah, he's turned into a werewolf, and he looks really hungry.

This was an actual recurring nightmare that haunted my childhood for years. I think the reason it so unnerved me was the unfairness of it. Sure, a kid expects to be torn apart by ferocious monsters that live *outside* in the woods or a cave or a pit. But it just doesn't seem right that the monsters can live in your own house—or be your own brother!

I think the reason idolatry gets so little attention today is that we are not truly convinced that it is something that's "inside the house." Like we saw in the last chapter, idolatry is something we think happens only in the jungle or in remote villages in developing nations. Idolatry is the stuff of *National Geographic*—not *USA Today.*

Sadly, most of today's spiritual diagnosticians do not include idolatry in the list of maladies threatening the church's health. Several other problems have been identified: declining church membership, unwholesome relationships, dysfunctional families, pornography—and the list goes on and on. But rarely, if ever, do we hear about our insatiable desire to trade in God for anything and everything. Whatever happened to idolatry? Frankly, we shouldn't be surprised that we so often feel immune to idolatry. The Scriptures warned us how easily we can be duped.

The Deceitfulness of Sin

The nightmare version of my brother seemed like a good guy. He helped me cordon off the bedroom and helped secure my safety. The things I feared were "out there," not in the sanctuary of my room. But nightmares are made of blind spots and poor judgments, aren't they? Had I been more alert, maybe I would have noticed Andy's face morphing into something wolfish before I was trapped.

The Bible is packed with warnings to look beneath the surface, to detect the slightest signs that something may be awry. Consider the following passages:

> *"Be careful," Jesus said to them. "Be on your guard against the yeast of the Pharisees and Sadducees."*
>
> Matthew 16:6 (NIV)

So be on your guard; *I have told you everything ahead of time.*
Mark 13:23 (NIV)

And he said to them, "Take care, and be on your guard *against all covetousness . . ."*
Luke 12:15

See to it that no one takes you captive by philosophy and empty deceit . . . (emphases added in preceding verses).
Colossians 2:8

P. T. Barnum allegedly said, "There's a sucker born every minute," and the Bible seems to agree. We are people who can be easily swindled. This is why the writer of Hebrews warns the church about the way sin works: "But exhort one another every day, as long as it is called 'today,' that none of you may be hardened by the deceitfulness of sin" (3:13).

Sin—idolatry in particular—is not a showboat. It does its best work in subtle ways. Like a puma lying low in the gentle grass, taut muscles held in place like a coiled spring, sin waits in the "safest" of places. If someone approached you and said, "Hey, I've got a bag full of idol statues. Would you like to trade Christ in for one of these?" then idolatry would be a pretty easy thing to resist. But remember what Ezekiel said: The capacity for idol worship is alive and well in our hearts. Sin knows this, so it waits patiently for a chance to creep in unaware. Consider the famous plight of the Israelites in their departure from Egypt.

Three Hots and a Cot

Ruthless Pharaoh horribly oppressed the Jewish people. Sensing a potential revolt, Pharaoh maniacally plotted a systematic extermination of the Jews, even ordering the slaughter of every Israelite boy

born in Egypt. The whole thing would have worked, too, had God
not made a nuisance of himself by showing up.

After many warnings through His servant Moses, God judged
the Egyptians by killing every firstborn son or animal (an ironic
reversal of Pharaoh's plan). He led the Israelites through the Red
Sea on a miraculously dry and dusty path. Then God capped it all
off by drowning the Egyptian army as it vainly pursued the Jews. It
was a great story! Well, it would have been, had it not been for those
nuisance Israelites.

Every nation has its skeletons in the closet. Israel's skeleton is
undoubtedly her whiny sniveling in the desert. Her awe of God's
miraculous power faded quickly as she waited in the wilderness for
the next step. In Egypt the Israelites had what modern prisoners call
"three hots and a cot"—three hot meals and a place to sleep. But
in the desert, they had no such security. All they had was Moses
telling them that God would be their provider. In one of the most
beautiful passages in Scripture, God describes His own perspective
on the Israelites' rescue. "You yourselves have seen what I did to the
Egyptians, and how I bore you on eagles' wings and brought you
to myself" (Exodus 19:4). Notice that God does not say, "I brought
you to *Mt. Sinai*." While that would have been geographically true,
it would not have emphasized the heart of the story. Instead, God
says, "I brought you to *myself*." This verse is a stunning picture of
God's power to break idolatry's death grip.

Once upon a time the Jews were enslaved to a "god" who gave
them something—three hots and a cot—in return for their bond-
age. The true God, however, crushed the one who had enslaved
them and gave the Israelites all they ever really needed—himself.
But notice what idolatry does; it convinces the Israelites that their
former "god" could satisfy them more than Yahweh. So they trade
God in for a pot of stew: "Now the rabble that was among them had

a strong craving. And the people of Israel also wept again and said, 'Oh that we had meat to eat! We remember the fish we ate in Egypt that cost nothing, the cucumbers, the melons, the leeks, the onions, and the garlic. But now our strength is dried up, and there is nothing at all but this manna to look at' " (Numbers 11:4–6).

Do you see the shift? "Sure, Pharaoh was a ruthless dictator, but he sure did know how to cook. Yes, God can part a sea, but He's not as good in the kitchen. After all, in Egypt we had pillows on the bed and potatoes in the pot."

When Blessings Become Bondage

It's interesting that what knocked Israel off track was something good: food. Who can read the Bible and come away with any other conclusion than that food is God's good gift to us? "He provides *food* for those who fear him; he remembers his covenant forever" (Psalm 111:5, emphasis added). Food is a good and wonderful thing; just ask my six-year-old daughter what she's feeling when she's standing in front of a make-your-own sundae bar! But even though food is a gift, the idolatry syndrome can still make God's blessing our burden.

When a woman's only motivation for getting through a workday is the anticipation of downing a pint of Ben and Jerry's when she gets home, something has gone wrong. When a high school student can't concentrate on the lesson because he's too busy fantasizing about his new Xbox game, something has gone wrong. When a husband's only interest in his wife is how she can satisfy him in bed, something has gone wrong. Yes, food, recreation, and sex are all good gifts of a gracious God. We rarely suspect that such things can serve as idolatry's playground, but remember, sin is deceitful. There is a blurry, almost imperceptible boundary line where God's gifts replace God himself. Let's return to our definition of idolatry:

cherishing, trusting, or fearing anything more than we cherish, trust, or fear God himself.

If a woman cannot find God's presence and power sufficient to sustain her through a day, then idolatry has hunted her down. If that student's Xbox fantasies shift from fun entertainment to ceaseless obsession, then idolatry has slipped through the back door and made itself at home. And when a husband stops seeing his wife as a God-given life partner and treats her only as an object for his own pleasure, then idolatry has done a good day's work. None of these victims may realize how deep in the throes of God-substitutes they actually are, but that's just fine with idolatry. Idolatry is a stealthy hunter.

Jesus tells a parable in Luke's gospel that captures how humans can be easily fooled by the apparent virtue of idols. Notice the things that impede people from coming to Christ.

> *But he said to him, "A man once gave a great banquet and invited many. And at the time for the banquet he sent his servant to say to those who had been invited, 'Come, for everything is now ready.' But they all alike began to make excuses. The first said to him, 'I have bought a field, and I must go out and see it. Please have me excused.' And another said, 'I have bought five yoke of oxen, and I go to examine them. Please have me excused.' And another said, 'I have married a wife, and therefore I cannot come' (Luke 14:16–20).*

It was not sex, drugs, or the insatiable lust for fame and fortune that prevented these would-be followers from going hard after Christ. No, idolatry is much too sly to come marching in with such flamboyance. The excuses offered are reasonable, and some might even say noble. John Piper offers a provocative observation of this passage.

The greatest enemy of hunger for God is not poison but apple pie. It is not the banquet of the wicked that dulls our appetite for heaven, but the endless nibbling at the table of the world. For all the ill that Satan can do, when God describes what keeps us from the banquet table of his love, it is a piece of land, a yoke of oxen, and a wife (Luke 14.18–20). The greatest adversary of love to God is not his enemies but his gifts. And the most deadly appetites are not for the poison of evil, but for the simple pleasures of earth. For when these replace an appetite for God himself, the idolatry is scarcely recognizable and almost incurable.[7]

A Glimmer of Hope?

I am thankful that Piper describes idolatry as "scarcely" recognizable and "almost" incurable. We have just spent five chapters considering the infectious power of the idolatry syndrome in the human soul. It's a frightening reality, isn't it? But now let's take Jesus at His word when He calls himself the Great Physician. We need Him to show us how to look for idolatry's symptoms. We need Him to show us how to eliminate the idols that have amassed like tumors in our hearts. But most of all we need Him—period. We need His beauty to shine brightly and expose our idols for the hollow impostors they are!

Prayer

Fight for us, O God, that we not drift numb and blind and foolish into vain and empty excitements. Life is too short, too precious, too painful to waste on worldly bubbles that burst. Heaven is too great, hell is too horrible, eternity is too long that

---

7. *A Hunger for God*, Wheaton, Illinois: Crossway Books, 1997.

we should putter around on the porch of eternity. O God, open our eyes to the vastness of the sufferings of Christ and what they mean for sin and holiness and hope and heaven. We fear our bent to trifling. Make us awake to the weight of glory—the glory of Christ's incomparable sufferings.

—John Piper

Study Guide

1. Read Hebrews 3:13. What images come to mind when you think of sin personified as deceitful? What are some everyday ways that we tend to let our guard down concerning the detection of sin in our lives?

2. Sometimes we make God's good gifts into idols. Note the first example and then fill in the rest.

God gives a gift.	We turn it into an idol.
Money	the measure of our happiness, security and success
Sex	
Children	
Spiritual gifts (teaching, wisdom, mercy)	

3. Read Matthew 6:24–34. How does this passage (and verse 33 in particular) help us draw a healthy boundary between the good things God gives us and the idols we insist on having?

Pacha: Uh-oh.

Kuzco: Let me guess.

We're about to go over a huge waterfall.

Pacha: Yep.

Kuzco: Sharp rocks at the bottom?

Pacha: Most likely.

Kuzco: . . . Bring it on.

—from Disney's *The Emperor's New Groove*

When God chastises his children, he does not punish
as a judge does; but he chastens as a father.

—Charles Spurgeon

My son, do not despise the Lord's discipline or be weary
of his reproof, for the Lord reproves him whom he loves,
as a father the son in whom he delights.

—Proverbs 3:11–12

relax, THINGS can only get worse

How Do You Love a Child Who's Dying?

Matthew was a marvelous, energetic boy, full of joy and mischief. At age seven he seemed to have experienced more life than half of the adults I knew. In the summer of 1992, I had the privilege of directing a summer camp where he won the hearts of everyone on staff. We loved this boy; most of us tried not to dwell on the fact that he had cystic fibrosis. No one knew how long Matthew had to live—three years, maybe seven. But Matthew didn't waste a minute of whatever time he had left. And we didn't miss a minute enjoying his presence among us. The counselors and I had an unspoken rule: *Don't let Matthew's mother know he had acted up unless his behavior was "off the charts" bad.* How does any decent person play a part in punishing a terminally ill child? Maybe a better question to ask is, "How do parents of dying children deal with the subject of discipline?"

Well, one hot August day, one "off the charts" day, I had to play the part I most dreaded: the tattletale. Matthew had gotten his hands on some paint (why children are ever allowed access to paint deserves a book all its own) and thought it would be amusing to do a little artwork on a few of the kids' backpacks. No way out of that one for the camp director—parents paying for camp don't like paying for replacement backpacks. When Matthew's mother came to pick him up that afternoon, I gathered all of my courage and tattled on a boy who would die in a few years.

His mother was calm and contemplative as I told the sordid tale. She thanked me, helped gather Matthew's things, and took the boy home. The next day she told me how he'd been punished. She sat him down at their kitchen table and told him that the allowance money he'd been saving for his Game Boy would now be used to replace the backpacks. She sent him to bed without dessert as well. Matthew cried, went to his room upset, and his mother never shed a tear—until she went into her bedroom, closed the door, and cried like she never had before. That is a picture of a mother's love.

Parents who love their children do them no favors by shielding them from the consequences of their actions, even when they are dying! What message would Matthew have gotten about his identity, his personhood, if his impending death made him immune to the moral laws of life? No, Matthew's mother knew that her boy needed to be protected from his callous attitudes toward fellow campers. She loved him, and it hurt! What a picture of God's fatherly love for us.

God's "No-Tolerance" Policy

There is a certain sense in which the rest of this book is unnecessary. For those of us who have come to faith in Christ, for those of us who now see Christ as the deepest satisfaction of our souls: God will not allow counterfeit saviors to rob us of His glory. Consider God's "no tolerance" policy of idols in the following passages.

- "I am the Lord your God, who brought you out of the land of Egypt, out of the house of slavery. You shall have no other gods before me. You shall not make for yourself a carved image . . . You shall not bow down to them or serve them, for I the Lord your God am a jealous God, visiting the iniquity of the fathers on the children to the third and the fourth generation of those who hate me" (Exodus 20:2–5).
- I am the Lord; that is my name; my glory I give to no other, nor my praise to carved idols (Isaiah 42:8).
- But first I will doubly repay their iniquity and their sin, because they have polluted my land with the carcasses of their detestable idols, and have filled my inheritance with their abominations (Jeremiah 16:18).

Even a cursory reading of the Bible makes it clear that God hates the counterfeits that seek to rival Him. Others have written on the subject of God's passion for His own glory,[8] and I do not need to review that discussion here. Suffice it to say that God knows that His own glory is the very thing our hearts are longing for. Perhaps the worst thing that could ever happen would be for God to allow us to find a false contentment in "gods" that cannot ultimately satisfy. No, God hates idols, and He loves us too much to leave us in their deceptively soothing embrace. Like Matthew's mother, He will hurt us to rescue us—if He must.

---

8. If it is not obvious to the reader already, I am indebted to the writings of John Piper. In my opinion, he has done more good for the church in calling attention to the supremacy of God in all things than any author alive today. I could not more highly recommend his signature work, *Desiring God*, where he skillfully unpacks the premise that "God is most glorified in us, when we are most satisfied in Him." All that I write on the harm idolatry brings to us is rooted in his observation that whatever God hates is harmful to us and whatever He loves is a blessing to us—especially His glory!

How God Rescues Us from Idolatry's Clutches

My wife and I are convinced that Chevy Chase's fictional Griswold family, the fated victims in the National Lampoon's Vacation movies, was not the right choice of family for those films. My wife and I should have been the first in line for the casting call. The first twenty-four hours of our first married vacation included the following "joys": a speeding ticket, a stomach bug, a lost pair of contacts, a sinus infection, and a lost credit card. Truthfully, it's made every vacation since seem like a tropical paradise. To this day, whenever we experience a "vacation obstacle," we encourage each other with the mantra, "Relax, things can only get worse."

Such Griswold experiences have forced us to evaluate what really matters in the Dutcher clan. Are we less of a family if we have horrible vacations? Is our entire year ruined by one comically tragic week in July? At times, we've been tempted to answer in the affirmative, but with a little perspective we know that we have much to be thankful for. In recent years, we have come to be convinced that God's love for us is in many ways measured by the obstacles we experience. To sever us from our idols and show us how much we have to be grateful for, God often lets things around us go haywire. It's as if He's saying to us, "Relax, things can only get worse."

Consider the example of Paul and his companions. Traveling the Roman Empire was no walk through the park. They experienced hunger, rejection, life-threatening attacks, sleeplessness, illness, and loneliness. Things got so bad sometimes that a number of critics suggested that God's blessing no longer rested on Paul and his crew. But in his second letter to the Corinthians, he reminds us that nothing could be further from the truth.

> *For we do not want you to be ignorant, brothers, of the affliction we experienced in Asia. For we were so utterly burdened beyond our strength that we despaired of life itself.*
>
> 2 Corinthians 1:8

Notice that rather than feeling ashamed of his obstacles, Paul wants them to know what a horrible time he was having. But why? Is he a masochist, a glutton for punishment, some poor misguided soul with a martyr's complex? The truth is that Paul sees something of the merciful discipline of God in his sufferings. Paul is convinced that his loving Father wants to free him from cherishing, trusting, or fearing something more than Christ. Notice what he says in the next verse.

> *Indeed, we felt that we had received the sentence of death. But that was to* make us rely not on ourselves but on God *who raises the dead* (emphasis added).
>
> 2 Corinthians 1:9

Paul is not on the "unlucky" side of a random, cosmic sledge-hammer. He is experiencing the sweet providence of God, which shows the apostle just how easily idols can creep into his life and steal the joy of resting in God alone. Think about it. How do you feel when you lose a night of sleep or stub your toe or misplace a twenty-dollar bill? Sleep, feet, and money are all good things, aren't they? But when losing or injuring these things makes your world fall apart, more precisely, makes *you* fall apart, doesn't that reveal something about what your heart has attached itself to? A seminary professor of mine had a helpful saying that I've never forgotten, "You know what your idols are by observing this: When they shake, you shake."

Am I cherishing, trusting in, or fearing the dwindling of my bank account? Then God loves me enough to send an unexpected bill in the mail perhaps. Do I trust too much in the compliments I receive? Then God may send me into a "dry season" where the most encouraging thing I hear is "Have a nice day" from the girl in the drive-through window. Paul's hardships were aimed to arrest his attention and soberly remind him that sleep, food, companionship, or any creature comfort were not enough to carry him through life. Such gifts become idols when we rely on them to bring us satisfaction. Paul needed one thing at the center, the same thing we need—Christ alone.

Relax, These Things Take Time

I preached on the subject of God's bringing our hidden idolatries to light a few years ago, only to be greeted by a tearful woman after church. "What you said is true, Greg. I'm ashamed that I've been a Christian for twenty years, and I still cherish, trust in, and fear so many things over Christ."

It's rare that I get a spontaneous burst of wisdom at just the right moment (probably to keep me from pride, the most subtle idol of all), but in this particular instance, to comfort this dear woman, I believe, God gave me just such a burst. "Margie," I asked, "do you think if Paul were alive today, he would be able to find a lot of areas in your life worthy of a good rebuke?"

Somewhat surprised by my bluntness, she balked, blushed, and murmured, "Probably."

I then pointed her to Philippians 3 and reminded her that Paul wrote this letter near the end of his life. I also reminded her of the things Paul experienced that Margie had not: seeing the risen Christ, hearing the audible voice of Christ, immediate and direct access to those who had walked with Christ, supernatural revelations of the third heaven (2 Corinthians 12)—all this to set the stage for a staggering confession from Paul's lips.

In this passage in Philippians 3 the apostle gives us his resume. Scholars have noted that if Paul's credentials could be transferred into a contemporary context, he would have the equivalent of two PhDs. But Paul's point is to show us how his credentials are nothing more than potential idols, things that are "rubbish" (literally "dung") compared to Christ.

But whatever was to my profit I now consider loss for the sake
of Christ. What is more, I consider everything a loss compared
to the surpassing greatness of knowing Christ Jesus my Lord,
for whose sake I have lost all things.

Philippians 3:7–8 NIV

Margie seemed confused at this point in the conversation.
Wasn't this comparison between her and Paul just making her feel
worse? Before more guilt could paralyze her, I jumped to the next
chapter. "Margie," I said, "read this verse."

I know what it is to be in need, and I know what it is to have
plenty. I have learned the secret of being content in any and
every situation, whether well fed or hungry, whether living in
plenty or in want.

Philippians 4:12 NIV

When I asked her what she thought Paul's "secret" to contentment was, she answered, "Christ—he just said so in the last
chapter."

"Right," I responded, "but was this his experience the whole
time he was a Christian?" After a few seconds, her eyes widened—
what a sweet sight that is in my memory still today—and I knew she
got it! Paul had to *learn* the secret. Bingo! Here's the apostle Paul,
a man probably none of us will ever come close to matching in his
love for God. And here, near the end of his life, he can share it: "I've
had to *learn* this," he says. God knows our frailty, our stubbornness,
our forgetfulness. But He will teach us the secret. If it took Paul
most of his life, then I say to you, "Relax, these things take time."

Prayer

Grant, Almighty God, as at the present time, thou dost deservedly chastise us for our sins, according to the example of thine ancient people, that we may turn our face to thee with true penitence and humility: May we throw ourselves suppliantly and prostrately before thee; and, despairing of ourselves, place our only hope in thy pity which thou hast promised.

—John Calvin

Study Guide

1. Read Isaiah 42:8 and Jeremiah 16:18. In light of these verses, how can we expect God to respond when we ignore idolatry at work in our lives?

2. Can you think of a situation in your life that was miserable at the time, but now you look back with thanksgiving as it was clearly evidence of God's loving discipline?

3. 2 Corinthians 1:8–9 tells us that hardships often serve as God's instrument for making us rely more on Him than ourselves. Interestingly, Paul gives a detailed list of the kinds of hardships he faced in 2 Corinthians 11:24–26. Take two of Paul's hardships and suggest what areas of his life God may have been working to refine.

4. How does the fact that Paul had to "learn" the secret of contentment (Philippians 4:12) affect you?

What I want out of each and every one of you is a
hard target search of every gas station, residence, warehouse,
farmhouse, henhouse, outhouse and doghouse in that area.
Checkpoints go up at fifteen miles. Your fugitive's name
is Doctor Richard Kimble. Go get him.
—from the movie *The Fugitive*

Many people live in darkness and ignorance about
their own hearts. They keep careful track of how their
investments are doing on Wall Street and get frequent checkups
at the doctor; they watch what they eat and work out at
the gym three or four times a week to keep their bodies finely
tuned. But how many people give the least thought to their souls?
If it is important to watch over and care for our bodies and
investments, which will soon die and rot, how much more
important is it for us to guard our immortal souls?
—Kris Lungaard

The heart is deceitful above all things, and desperately sick;
who can understand it?
—Jeremiah 17:9

doing a
diagnostic

Symptoms That Hide from Us

In chapter 6 we saw that idolatry is a stealthy hunter. Like a curfew-violating teenager, it knows how to walk up the staircase without making the floorboards squeak. Should it surprise us, then, that the symptoms of idolatry know how to go underground?

Try this exercise for a moment. Take out a piece of paper and pen and ask yourself this question: "In what four areas of my life is idolatry at work right now?" Now, write them down. If you're having a good day, maybe one area came to mind. If it's a really good day, maybe you could name two, but I doubt you were able to identify the areas specifically. In other words, maybe you said that idolatry is at work in your job—but *just where exactly* in your job is idolatry doing its dirty work? Are you frustrated that your boss or co-workers are not affirming you? Are you obsessed with the fact that you're not making a fair salary? Are you constantly preoccupied with your last performance rating? Or maybe it's as simple as wanting a better parking place? And here's what's even more aggravating: Even when you ask such explicit questions, idolatry still doesn't step forward and expose itself. It just doesn't play fair!

My childhood friend Rob claimed to be the greatest Marco Polo player in the neighborhood, but his self-appointed title was always in dispute. Why? He played dirty. When ten or twelve pre-adolescents play this game in a small pool, everyone should get tagged eventually. The leader closes his eyes and counts to ten. He then calls out "Marco," and the other kids respond "Polo." The leader locates the others by tracking the sounds of their voices. No matter how much you dodged and weaved, sooner or later your voice gave you away. Unless you were Rob. This kid was slick, and he knew how to mouth the word "Polo" without ever using his vocal cords. The same could be said about our idols. No amount of wishful thinking will bring them to the surface. When we call "Marco," they stay as quiet as cheating Rob did years ago in that neighborhood pool. In truth, there is only one way to detect idols. It's really the same way to detect a childhood cheater—we have to keep our eyes open.

Open Our Eyes, Lord

Have you ever noticed how packed the gospels are with stories of blindness? Jesus heals a staggering number of people who were afflicted with this disease. Consider the following examples.

> *As Jesus passed on from there, two blind men followed him, crying aloud, "Have mercy on us, Son of David!" When he entered the house, the blind men came to him, and Jesus said to them, "Do you believe that I am able to do this?" They said to him, "Yes, Lord."*
>
> Matthew 9:27–28

> *Then a demon-oppressed man who was blind and mute was brought to him, and he healed him, so that the man spoke and saw.*
>
> Matthew 12:22

*In that hour [Jesus] healed many people of diseases and plagues
and evil spirits, and on many who were blind he bestowed
sight.*

Luke 7:21

Why so many stories (many more than the ones listed here)
about the blind receiving sight? I mean, sure, it's a great event, but
it doesn't come close to raising people from the dead. And line for
line there are far more stories about the blind than the resuscitated. I
am convinced that the gospel writers wanted us to *see* something far
greater than the restoration of physical sight in these stories, something greater that ocular vision only points to. The most extended
account of a blind man's healing is found in the ninth chapter of
John's gospel.

The disciples come across a man who has been blind from birth.
Like most of us, tragedy moves them to curiosity. "Rabbi, who
sinned, this man or his parents, that he was born blind?" (v. 2). And
unlike most of us, Jesus is moved to action by this tragedy. "It was
not that this man sinned, or his parents, but that the works of God
might be displayed in him. We must work the works of him who
sent me while it is day; night is coming, when no one can work"
(vv. 3–4). Jesus makes it clear that now is not the time for a theological discussion; it's time to glorify the Father by restoring this man's
sight, which is exactly what Jesus does. But unlike the recorders of
the other blindness accounts, John parks on the aftermath of this
miracle for an entire chapter. (You may want to put this book down
and come back when you've finished John 9. It's one of the wittiest
and subtlest passages in all of Scripture.)

The rest of the passage depicts the blind man's conflict with the
religious professionals of Jesus' day, the Pharisees. While we might
expect them to throw the blind man a party for his restored sight,

they put him on the hot seat. *He did this on the Sabbath? Were you really ever blind in the first place? What—you don't think this guy is a prophet, do you?* The formerly blind man merely stands his ground and says that Jesus healed him, pure and simple. But why does John devote so much space to this aftermath? The answer comes in the last section, when Jesus re-enters the picture.

Having heard that the Pharisees have excommunicated the blind man, Jesus pays him a visit. The Savior asks the man if he believes that Jesus is the Son of Man (in other words, the Messiah). The man responds that he does believe. Then Jesus utters these sobering words: "For judgment I came into this world, that those who do not see may see, and those who see may become blind" (v. 39). The man's physical vision is really just a metaphor for something greater: his spiritual understanding. Conversely, the Pharisees whose physical eyes are fine are spiritually blind. There is a kind of seeing that only Jesus can grant, a seeing that detects Jesus for who he really is and detects sin for what it really is. As believers in Christ, we have access to this kind of sight, but rarely do we use it.

The idolatry syndrome has enjoyed an almost invisible status in most Christian communities today. One of the reasons I wrote this book is because I just can't find much material on the subject. Os Guinness has deftly pointed out our silence on the subject.

> Idolatry is the most discussed problem in the Bible and one of the most powerful spiritual and intellectual concepts in the believer's arsenal. Yet for Christians today it is one of the least meaningful notions and is surrounded with ironies. Perhaps this is why many evangelicals are ignorant of the idols in their lives. Contemporary evangelicals are little better at recognizing and resisting idols than modern secular people are. There can be no believing communities

without an unswerving eye to the detection and destruction of idols.[9]

The time has come for Christians to rediscover the tools for detecting the symptoms of idolatry.

The Tired Old Dynamic Duo

Let me first put forth two shocking statements:

1. Reading the Bible will not expose our idols.
2. Praying will not expose our idols.

What? Have you ever read a Christian book that devalued the role of Bible reading and prayer as a solution to something? To even hint at this might approach heresy. But let's examine the statements more closely to see why they are true.

First, Bible reading in itself does not have the power to expose our idols. Think of various people who might read the Bible for different reasons: atheistic philosophers, Hollywood filmmakers, *New York Times* crossword buffs, the Pharisees! There is ample evidence that mere Bible reading does not guarantee the exposure (let alone the eventual uprooting) of idols. Bible reading by itself can be a great task, but at root it is about information: *What does it say? Where did it happen? Who was involved?* But the people who want to get serious about bringing their idols into the light want more than information; they want transformation.

Second, prayer in itself does not have the power to expose our idols. Again, think of various people who pray for many reasons: the desperate gambler rooting for the gray horse, the famished father absently rushing through a mantra before diving into the gravy bowl, the dutiful Sunday school student who puts in his weekly request

9. *Fit Bodies Fat Minds*. Grand Rapids, Michigan: Baker Publishing Group, 1994.

for healing for Aunt Martha's bunions, the Pharisees! Prayer—even long, *King James*-style prayer—is no guarantee that our idols will come into the light. More often than not, prayer can actually be twisted into a request for *more* idols!

So if Bible reading and prayer are not the answers, just how do we detect the subtle symptoms of idolatry? Well, I must confess that I've played a little dirty myself in this chapter. There is a way that Bible reading and prayer do work to unveil our idols, but let me propose a more carefully worded third statement.

3. Prayerful Bible reading will expose our hidden idols.

Psalm 119: The Believer's Night Goggles

The author of Psalm 119 loves the Bible. Every verse references the Scriptures by one term or another. *Laws, precepts, statutes, commands*—such things are the delight of the psalmist. In fact, his experience is evidence that the Bible can empower us to live holy, righteous lives.

> *How can a young man keep his way pure? By guarding it according to your word.*
>
> Verse 9

> *I have stored up your word in my heart, that I might not sin against you.*
>
> Verse 11

> *I hold back my feet from every evil way, in order to keep your word.*
>
> Verse 101

But don't these verses disprove the first statement, that reading the Bible will not expose our idols? They would if Psalm 119 were about reading the Bible—but it isn't. This psalm is about *basking* in the Bible. Notice how the psalmist describes his experience with the Scripture; *reading* is not the right word.

In the way of your testimonies I delight as much as in all riches.

Verse 14

I will delight in your statutes; I will not forget your word.

Verse 16

I open my mouth and pant, because I long for your commandments.

Verse 131

The psalmist reads the Bible with a prayerful heart. He is not interested merely in information, but transformation. When he reads a passage on adultery, he lets his mind soak in the words like a sponge, all the while asking the Lord to expose any lust in his heart. If he reads a verse about jealousy, his heart pleads for God to shine the spotlight on the green-eyed monster before it topples him. If he reads a passage describing Israel's grumbling, he sits with the passage, allowing the Spirit of God to expose the complaining spirit in his own heart. When he gets serious about detecting idols, he doesn't read the Bible without praying, and he doesn't pray without having an open Bible in front of him. No matter how hard they try, idols cannot find a safe place to hide from this kind of prayerful immersion in Scripture. Interestingly, the psalmist asks to be released from idols in this prayer:

Turn my eyes from looking at worthless things; and give me life in your ways.

Verse 37

Worthless things—counterfeit saviors, false gods, idols. The things that promise us satisfaction but leave us with nothing. There's only one way to expose them: by prayerfully reading the Scripture.

BBC news recently reported that movie theater ushers are beginning to catch up with criminals who illegally record feature films with concealed video equipment. How do you catch these ruffians with such miniature but sophisticated recorders in a dark, crowded theater? Easy—with night goggles. These high-tech spectacles can detect the tiniest rays of lights from handheld camcorders. Imagine what these crafty criminals must experience when a teenage movie usher with night goggles taps them on the shoulder! If we are serious about detecting the tiniest rays of light from the glitter and shine of our idols, then let's join with David, another psalmist, and say, "Search me, O God, and know my heart! Try me and know my thoughts! And see if there be any grievous way in me, and lead me in the way everlasting" (139:23–24).

Prayer

Keep me from deception by causing me to abide in the truth, from harm by helping me to walk in the power of the Spirit. Lord, help me, for I am often lukewarm and chill; unbelief mars my confidence, sin makes me forget Thee. Let the weeds that grow in my soul be cut at their roots; grant me to know that I truly live only when I live to Thee, that all else is trifling.

—from The Valley of Vision

Study Guide

1. Why do you think idolatry receives so little attention in the church today? Do you think it should be addressed more often?

2. Do you agree that simply reading the Bible or simply praying is not sufficient to expose our idols? How do verses like Psalm 139:23–24 and Hebrews 4:12–13 help us better understand the *kind* of reading and praying we should be engaged in?

3. Can you share some examples in your own life where God has exposed your idols through prayer or Scripture reading? What are some ways that Christians in fellowship (church, prayer groups, small groups) could lovingly help one another discover idols in their lives?

Know when to walk away and know when to run.
—Kenny Rogers, *The Gambler*

A carved image cannot forgive, save, give peace of mind,
or solve problems; nor can money, fame, education,
social prestige, or any other such thing that men come to trust in.
Every idol is man-made, and every idol is helpless to help.
Idols only defile. They never glorify God but always dishonor
Him. Since no good can come of idolatry, the only
response to it should be to flee.
—John MacArthur

Little children, keep yourselves from idols.
—1 John 5:21

ready, set . . .
retreat!

How Unmanly Is That?

"Go ahead, make my day."

"Do you feel lucky, punk?"

"Don't make me angry—you wouldn't like me when I'm angry."

These are some of the beloved quotes of boys from my generation. Each of us wanted to be the guy who was always in control, never afraid, unflinchingly committed to staring the enemy down until he tucked his tail and ran. Our heroes were rugged cops, unshaven rebels, and mysterious outcasts. Rarely did we stop and consider the irony of our context. We were the boys of middle class suburbia. We watched shows and movies featuring these kinds of tough characters on long summer afternoons in a house where one of our moms was busy making us a tray of cookies and Kool-Aid. Our dads were mailmen, accountants, insurance salesman, and in the case of my own . . . a librarian!

There were not a lot of villains to confront in the quiet book aisles of the Parkville library. The most exciting thing to happen might be the occasional mis-shelved novel in the nonfiction section.

Amazingly, though, my mild-mannered father taught me one of the most valuable lessons of combat. I had a severe speech impediment throughout most of my childhood. It's a brutal but inevitable fact of life that many kids smelled blood in the midst of my stuttering, and the bullies were always ready to attack in a moment's notice. Pushes, jabs, threats, and name-calling were part and parcel of a typical school day for such a stammering kid. In a movie, my dad would have sat me down and given me one of those cool pep talks where I was told to stand up and take it out of some bully's hide. But I still remember my dad's sage advice: "Greg, some kids are just plain jerks. You could fight them, win sometimes, lose sometimes. But here's what I think you should do: Walk away."

It didn't sound very manly to me at the time, but as I've aged I have seen my father live by this rule with great success. He is a man who has stayed faithful to his wife for forty years, has an excellent relationship with his children and grandchildren, and is revered by many of his peers. So maybe he knows something about life. Maybe he's tapped into a secret that's far more significant then he realizes.

The Best Offense Is a Good Defense

In the next chapter we will look at a more offensive strategy in dealing with idolatry, but in this one we will consider an often overlooked maxim of warfare: *The best offense is a good defense.* Ask a talented football coach what wins games—not the glamorous momentum of an offensive drive, as necessary as that is, but the slow, steady plodding along of the defensive squad play after play. The Scriptures call us to be primarily defensive in our posture toward idols. Consider these two passages, the clearest, most succinct commands to the believer concerning idolatry.

Therefore, my beloved, flee from idolatry.
1 Corinthians 10:14

Little children, keep yourselves from idols.

1 John 5:21

It's interesting: Even though each command was written by two different men (first Paul then John), they have some striking similarities. Both of them speak affectionately to the church, using phrases that speak of love and concern: *beloved* and *little children.* Why are warnings against idolatry couched in such sweet, sentimental terms? I learned the answer recently by observing a conversation between my wife and our six-year-old daughter.

"Mommy, you never want me to talk with strangers, right?" Samantha asked.

"That's right, honey," Lisa replied.

"There are some people who aren't nice, who would hurt kids, right Mommy?"

I didn't need to be a mind reader to know that my wife's heart was breaking as she witnessed one of many "coming-of-age" moments in her daughter's life. Lisa fiercely held back her tears, forced a gentle smile (so full of tenderness it makes my heart break just remembering it), and calmly replied, "That's right, baby. But we pray that God protects us everyday. And don't ever talk to strangers, okay?"

The apostles viewed themselves as parents[10] more than supervisors. Knowing the great harm that idols can inflict upon us, they urge us to steer clear of them at every turn. We learn something humbling about ourselves in these commands, don't we? As much as we'd like to be spiritual "Dirty Harrys," idols are powerful forces

---

10. A striking example of such parental imagery is found in Paul's first letter to the Thessalonians. In chapter 2:7 he writes, "We were gentle among you, like a nursing mother taking care of her own children. So, being affectionately desirous of you, we were ready to share with you not only the gospel of God but also our own selves, because you had become very dear to us." If Jesus is our Savior, He has already borne the wrath we deserve for our idolatry (see chapter 4), but God urges us, as a loving parent, to pursue what's best for us.

that are not to be cavalierly taunted. My dad knew that my getting tangled up in a never-ending conflict with bullies (some of which could have landed me in the hospital) was not going to help me grow into the man I was destined to become. So he urged me— wisely urged me—to run like the wind when I could. No one would say that the God of Scripture is a wimp, would they? He is, as one scholar puts it, "the Divine Warrior." Nevertheless, He deems it wise to run when we can.[11]

> Flee *from sexual immorality.*
>
> 1 Corinthians 6:18

> But as for you, O man of God, flee *these things. Pursue righteousness, godliness, faith, love, steadfastness, gentleness.*
>
> 1 Timothy 6:11

> So flee *youthful passions and pursue righteousness, faith, love, and peace, along with those who call on the Lord from a pure heart* (emphasis added in all preceding verses).
>
> 2 Timothy 2:22

The Christian life is not a one-time charge up the enemy's embankment, a do-or-die mission where we run purely on adrenaline. Yes, there are times when we do commit ourselves to such attacks, but we won't last long if that's all we do. Retreating allows us time to regroup, to assess what's important, to determine how to navigate through a difficult situation. Let's think through two examples.

Idolatry and Thirty-One Flavors

Bill finally sees that he has attached far too much importance to eating. Those cravings to pull over and get something sweet have

---

11. Tremper Longman, *God Is a Warrior.* Grand Rapids, Michigan: Zondervan, 1995.

moved from an occasional time-out to a daily event. The Lord graciously reveals to Bill that he is hurting his body and his time with his family. (He's spending extended lunch breaks at Baskin Robbins and actually has to work late as a result.) The final straw that convinced him of his problem was the onset of a horribly angry mood when he realized he'd forgotten his wallet one day and would not be able to get his lunchtime treat. His idol, ice cream, was shaken, and Bill was shaking along with it. Christ could have been his satisfaction, extended time with his Savior could have been his "treat," but the idolatry syndrome has rushed in and played Bill for a sucker.

How does Bill handle his problem? Does he walk into Baskin Robbins and stare at the oh-so-tempting thirty-one bins of enticement and fight the urge to eat? Such an act would be suicide, not sanctification. In Bill's case, fleeing might be equivalent to leaving his spare change (credit cards, if necessary!) at home. Maybe it's as radical as taking a different route where he doesn't pass the temple of frozen delights. Whatever it takes to avoid his idol is the best thing Bill could do.

Idolatry in the Book Club

Janet has made the Tuesday night book club discussion her most important moment of the week. For the summer, they are discussing three novels by Jody Picoult, her favorite, and she just loves the interaction among the ladies who attend. What started as a refreshing pastime has now become an addiction. She didn't even realize that the idolatry syndrome had done its work when her husband was given a free place to stay in the mountains for three days, Monday through Wednesday. Janet and Mark had not been on a trip alone in years, and Mark was eager to get some alone time with his wife. But Janet couldn't miss the book club that week; they were discussing *The Pact*, her favorite. Mark begged her to go away with him, even offered to discuss the book with her (yes, ladies, you can tell this is a fictional example), but Janet could not let go.

Weeks later, she had been spending good time, "Psalm 119" time, in her Bible (see the last chapter), and she *saw* it—her book club was giving her what only Jesus should: an identity, a purpose, a joy. How should she handle it? Should she run to the store to buy Ms. Picoult's newest novel, only to stand in front of it and chant, "I will not read this now. I will first spend time with the Lord, then with Mark, then with the kids. *I will not read this now. I will not read . . .*" Maybe it's just time for Janet to take a hiatus from her obsession. Again, please note that there is nothing wrong with reading a good book for enjoyment, but the boundary line between enjoyment and enslavement is hard to discern sometimes, isn't it? Janet's best move would be to see just how much her book addiction is hurting her and run like the wind in the other direction.

So maybe my wise, librarian father was right about running. There are things in this world that are too dangerous, too alluring to get too close to. Such things might enslave us and hold us back from experiencing the greatest joy we could ever know. And finally, to that joy we now turn.

Prayer

Save me from the love of the world and the pride of life, from everything that is natural to fallen man, and let Christ's nature be seen in me day by day. Grant me grace to bear Thy will without repining, and delight to be not only chiselled, squared, or fashioned, but separated from the old rock where I have been embedded so long, and lifted from the quarry to the upper air, where I may be built in Christ for ever.

—The Valley of Vision

Study Guide

1. Read 1 Corinthians 10:14. What strategy does this verse tell us to take in regard to idols? Describe a fictional situation where someone "fights" an idol. How does this approach fail?

2. Can you think of biblical examples where a righteous person fled from sin or where a righteous person was commanded to flee? (Hint: Don't forget about that pillar of salt thing—but think of some more besides this.) Can you think of a biblical example of a righteous person who did not flee and failed?

3. Can you think of other present-day examples where the only way to fight idolatry is to flee? How could such a "retreat" glorify God's worth in the eyes of an unbelieving world?

We're more popular than Jesus Christ now.
—John Lennon, in *Time*, August 12, 1966

Christ is a jewel worth more than a thousand worlds, as all know
who have him. Get him, and get all; miss him and miss all.
—Thomas Brooks

He is the image of the invisible God, the firstborn of all creation.
For by him all things were created, in heaven and on earth,
visible and invisible, whether thrones or dominions or rulers
or authorities—all things were created through him and for him.
And he is before all things, and in him all things hold together.
And he is the head of the body, the church. He is
the beginning, the firstborn from the dead, so that
in everything he might be preeminent.
—Colossians 1:15–18

cherishing
CHRIST for who
he is

A House on the Beach

For the past several years we have had the privilege of vacationing at a beautiful oceanfront house in Bethany Beach, Delaware. It's a perfect arrangement; a "friend-of-a-friend" connection to the owners allows me to park our family every summer at this beautiful piece of property—for free! Do I love this house? You betcha. It allows me to be close to everything: the sand, the surf, the boardwalk, the concession stands—all the necessary components of a successful beach vacation. But if the house had a soul, it would probably despise me. Why? Because I like it only for what I get out of it.

If this attractive home were in the middle of an Iowa cornfield, I would have no interest in it. The fact of the matter is that I use the house at Bethany as a means to an end. If the house ever lost its connection to the fringe benefits surrounding it, I'd start looking for a new house.

I have a real fear about the current state of Christian communities today. My concern is that for all of our songs, books, sermons, seminars, bumper stickers, and trinkets, Jesus is little more than "a house on the beach." He's great when He can get us this thing or that. Take some time and surf some church Web sites sometime and take note of what you find. There are many sermons about Jesus, but most of them treat Him as a *means* to something else. Jesus shows us how to handle stress, deal with fear, cope with change, overcome anger, or succeed in relationships. Few of them are about the depth of beauty found in Jesus himself. Is it any wonder that new Christians are usually so full of joy and exuberance? The fringe benefits of being connected to Jesus—heaven, forgiveness, a soothed conscience—are all fresh and alive to the new believer. Like the house at Bethany Beach, Jesus gets us close to the "good stuff" that puts a smile on our face.

Now don't get me wrong. The Scriptures sanction an appropriate celebration of the benefits of salvation (for example in Luke 15, where there is a lavish party for the return of the prodigal son). But these things were never meant to become the substance of our life in Christ. Can you imagine a party that lasted seventy years? Who could endure it! No, the Christian hope is rooted in one thing: an absolute preoccupation with the beauty of Christ himself. Not a preoccupation with the benefits Christ brings, but with Jesus himself. Until we are convinced that Jesus is a treasure in himself, for no other reason than for being who He is, we will continue to turn our hearts to the copies and counterfeits that offer us "fresher" benefits.

If It's True About Coffee . . .

I recently came across a book with a wonderful title for a Starbucks junkie like me, *Coffee: Discovering, Exploring, Enjoying.*[12]

---

12. Hattie Ellis and Debbie Treolar. London: Ryland Peters and Small Ltd., 2002.

There is obviously an audience for coffee in America, so much so that an entire book can invite the reader into a lifelong process of discovering all of coffee's treasures. How much more could an endless line of books, albums, or paintings be devoted to discovering, exploring, and enjoying Jesus Christ![13] Scottish theologian Sinclair Ferguson offers this diagnosis/prognosis in light of the church's current condition: "The evangelical orientation is inward and subjective. We are far better at looking inward than we are at looking outward. Instead, we need to expend our energies admiring, exploring, expositing, and extolling Jesus Christ."[14]

Being enamored with Christ is the best offensive weapon against idolatry. When idols call for our attention, we should flee, yes, but in fleeing we need to ask God to show us the excellencies of the Savior. Hearts that cherish, trust, or fear Jesus more than anything else prove to be barren soil for idols. Counterfeit saviors cannot grow in soil that has been reserved for Christ alone. But how are we to stir up mighty and glorious thoughts of Christ?

Again . . . Cynthia: A Champion of Beholding Christ

In chapter 2 I described a dear woman named Cynthia. You remember—the one who got the bad news about her cancer. What I didn't tell you was that Cynthia was one of those rare people who knew that the heart of the Christian life was all about beholding Christ for who He is. Days before she died we had a conversation I consider to be among the most sacred I have ever had. Let me take you there with me for just a moment.

---

13. It has been encouraging to see some recent works devoted solely to this purpose: John Piper's *Seeing and Savoring Jesus Christ*; Kris Lundgaard's *Through the Looking Glass*, and the late Rich Mullins' *Jesus Record*. Would that there be an avalanche of such works in the near future! It's time to balance the scales.

14. As quoted in C. J. Mahaney, *The Cross Centered Life*. Sisters, Oregon: Multnomah, 2002.

I enter the small hospice room and find Cynthia in a chair looking out the window, her back turned to me. Upon closer inspection, I see that she's not looking out the window; her eyes are closed. On the sill next to her is a small boom box; a BeBe and CeCe Winans worship song pours from its speakers. Cynthia's hands are lifted in the air, and tears of joy roll down her cheeks. I start to speak only to catch myself. How could I interrupt this moment? A dying woman is communing with her Savior, the Savior who will look into her face just days from now. I simply stand, awestruck by what I see. When the song ends, I come up behind her and gently squeeze her shoulder. She turns, smiles at me—as if she knew I was there all along—and invites me to talk with her about what she read that morning. I don't know that what she is about to share will change the course of my life . . .

She had read Luke 7:11–14. At the time, probably neither of us knew that this story is found only in Luke's gospel. For whatever reason, the other gospel writers did not feel a need to include it in their accounts. And certainly neither of us knew that in a week's time I would be preaching from this very passage at Cynthia's funeral.

Soon afterward [Jesus] went to a town called Nain, and his disciples and a great crowd went with him. As he drew near to the gate of the town, behold, a man who had died was being carried out, the only son of his mother, and she was a widow, and a considerable crowd from the town was with her. And when the Lord saw her, he had compassion on her and said to her, "Do not weep." Then he came up and touched the bier, and the bearers stood still. And he said, "Young man, I say to you, arise!" And the dead man sat up and began to speak, and Jesus gave him to his mother (Luke 7:11–14).

The passage had deeply impacted Cynthia because, unlike in most miracle accounts, Jesus does not follow up with a teaching moment or a call to commitment. He simply passes through a town, sees a woman's pain, raises her son, and (the most striking aspect of the story to Cynthia) gives "him to his mother." Cynthia was convinced that God put this passage in the Bible for no other reason than for us to see "just how beautiful Jesus is," her exact words. And as far as I'm concerned, her final words.

Everything we talked about from that moment on was just a sub-point of that larger theme—the beauty of Christ. From that moment on, the thrust of my ministry was forever changed. I would devote myself to calling attention to Christ's glory, beauty, worth, wisdom, majesty, love, power, gentleness, humility, joy, simplicity, and, as we can see, there simply are not enough words to describe Him. But the more I immerse myself in contemplating just how beautiful, strong, precious, and awesome my Savior is, the less and less appealing my idols look.

Jesus Is Greater Than . . .

If I could offer you "tips and techniques" for cherishing Christ more than anything else, then this book could have been a simple tract or pamphlet. The challenge, however, is that beholding Christ is a lifetime process. It involves a commitment to spending time with Him and following hard after Him. It assumes a lifelong passion to delve into Scripture and explore Christ's character. I can do little more than introduce you to a journey, a journey to explore why Jesus Christ is more precious than anything.

I love to break out old hymnals and read the words older writers used to describe Christ. Here's a favorite you may know.

Fairest Lord Jesus!
Ruler of all nature!
O Thou of God and man the Son!
Thee will I cherish,
Thee will I honor,
Thou my soul's glory, joy and crown!

Fair are the meadows,
Fairer still the woodlands,
Robed in the blooming garb of spring:
Jesus is fairer,
Jesus is purer,
Who makes the woeful heart to sing.

Fair is the sunshine,
Fairer still the moonlight,
And all the twinkling starry host:
Jesus shines brighter,
Jesus shines purer
Than all the angels heaven can boast.

Beautiful Savior!
Lord of all the nations!
Son of God and Son of Man!
Glory and honor,
Praise, adoration
Now and forever more be Thine!

Notice how this hymn invites us to contemplate Christ's superiority to everything—sun, moon, stars, anything of beauty in the natural world. This is how we go on the offense against idolatry. We tell everything that competes for our trust, fear, and affections that Jesus is greater. When we don't feel that He is greater in our hearts, we flee from the idols and ask God to show us the surpassing beauty of His Son. And then one day, this battle with idolatry will be over and done: "But we know that when he appears we shall be like him, because we shall see him as he is" (1 John 3:2).

What will strike the final deathblow to idolatry's presence? Yes, seeing the face of Christ when we behold Him face to face. Until that day, we can pray the following prayer.

Prayer

O Lord our God, grant us grace to desire Thee with our whole heart; that, so desiring, we may seek, and seeking find Thee; and so finding Thee may love Thee; and loving Thee, may hate those sins from which Thou hast redeemed us.

—Anselm

Study Guide

1. In your own experience, have you seen that Jesus is too often presented as a "house on the beach?" In what ways have you treated Jesus like this?

2. Why do you think it is so difficult for us to think of Jesus as a treasure in himself?

3. Read Philippians 3:10. What is it about this verse that tells you that Jesus was a treasure *in himself* to Paul—not merely a means to an end?

4. Glance through appendix B and the recommended readings and share some of the books, verses, songs, or quotes that most help you in treasuring Jesus Christ more than idols. Are there others that help you that aren't listed in this book?

Idolatry Syndrome Case Studies: Cherishing Christ More Than Stuff or Sex

As a pastor, I love to present a spiritual truth from Scripture, and I realize how important it is (sometimes because I forget and people in my congregation remind me) to "put a handle on it." If we aren't taught how to apply spiritual truth, it's somewhat like convincing a person that she needs to take a certain medicine to counteract an ingested poison. The dying person desperately says, "Give me that antidote," only to be told, "Oh . . . um . . . I'm not sure where you can find it."

This chapter aims at being a sort of "handle" (or "antidote," if you'd prefer) for you to grab. If you finish this book and say, "I'm convinced. Idolatry is a major problem in my life, and I want to cherish Christ more than anything," then I'm thrilled. But if you're left wondering, "Now what do I do?" you may just get frustrated. That would be tragic.

Let's put on our "biblical scrubs" and examine four case studies in idolatry: two about stuff and two about sex. These are broad categories, but they are potentially everyday idols for the follower of Christ. Learning to resist their influence will better prepare us to battle the countless gods that daily bombard us as twenty-first-century Christians.

Cherishing Christ More Than Stuff

Case Study #1: Bruce and Tammy against Sony and Brazilian Hardwood

Patient Background: Young, happily married newlyweds. Both work full-time in satisfying jobs, and they own their first home: a quaint condo. While this committed, Christian couple is not wealthy, they have been blessed, materially speaking, with everything they need.

Profile: Bruce and Tammy are happy with their quaint condo; it's a perfect starter home for a young couple. Their good friends, Jay and Laura, also newlyweds, just invited them over to their new house. That's right—a house, not a condo!

Just pulling into the driveway proves to be a battle for Bruce and Tammy. *Is that a home or the governor's mansion*, they think. Walking up to the front door, they notice a sign on the perfectly trimmed front lawn: "This lawn is cared for by The Lovely Lawn Company." Keeping a plastic smile on their faces, they do the mental math and determine that the cost just to upkeep the grounds must at least rival their two car payments. Jay and Laura open the door, but little do they know that their good friends who greet them are already starting to despise them.

The tour of the five-bedroom colonial home proves too enormously difficult for Bruce and Tammy. He can't get his mind off the Sony, 52-inch flat screen TV that hangs on the wall like a picture—a picture of NFL live-action glory, that is! She, on the other hand, has thought little of the television. How could she? Her eyes can't seem to break the spell the Brazilian hardwood floors have cast on her. Who knew Brazil had such gorgeous hardwood!

Now Bruce and Tammy are committed Christians, so they know exactly how to interact with Jay and Laura. As they tour the house, Bruce smiles at all the right moments and offers the appropriate "Praise-the-Lord," "What-a-blessing," and "God-is-good" sentiments in a spirit of "encouragement." Tammy cocks her head with a smile in that "I couldn't be more interested" manner when Laura tells her the detailed story of how they finally came to choose this type of hardwood.

An outside observer would undoubtedly declare this get-together a smashing success: Christians rejoicing in the blessings that come to their brothers and sisters in Christ. But an inside man—that is, one who could look deep into Bruce and Tammy's hearts—would see the truth. Idolatry has nestled down deep into their souls.

When they return home that night, their little condo has lost its quaint charm. Their former piece of paradise now seems like a run-down shanty. As Bruce puts a few dishes in the sink before going to bed, he realizes how small the kitchen is. Sure, Tammy has always been fond of calling it *cozy*, but tonight Bruce thinks *cramped* is a better adjective. The walls seem to close in on him like a trash-compactor. *Call me Luke Skywalker*, he thinks, recollecting the suspenseful scene from the first *Star Wars* movie.

Tammy is in the bathroom brushing her teeth. *Only one sink in here—that's crazy*, she determines. Every bathroom in the *palace*—that's what Tammy decided to call Laura's house within ten seconds of setting her eyes on it—had a double sink. *Bruce and I are always busy, always running against the clock. We should have a double sink.*

A few hours later, Bruce is awakened by the muffled sounds very close to him. Switching on the bedside lamp, he sees his young wife sitting upright, clutching a pillow.

"Honey?" he asks. "What's wrong?"

"I'm ashamed, Bruce." Fighting back tears to the point where she can speak somewhat clearly, she confesses everything.

In vivid detail, Tammy tells her husband that she's gone through a range of emotions since seeing their friend's home earlier in the evening. From shock to confusion, from envy to anger, from greed to self-pity, she pours out her soul. She knows that as a believer in Christ, she is to be content in Christ alone. Just this past Sunday, the pastor's message was on Paul's life's passion in Philippians 3:10: "that I may know him and the power of his resurrection, and may share his sufferings, becoming like him in his death." It had resonated deeply in Tammy's heart, and she decided, *That's the kind of woman I want to be.*

"But all it took was one look at Laura's floors, and all of a sudden, I felt empty. Like I was being deprived of something. What's wrong with me, honey?"

Bruce pauses. His instinct is to say something really spiritual, as if he hasn't been fantasizing all night about having a TV like Jay's. *Well, that's not entirely true*, he thinks, *I was actually dreaming of a bigger one—one that would make Jay's look like a kid's View-Master.* It dawns on Bruce that he can't deny it any longer.

"Tammy, I'm right there with you, honey. I was so envious I was just waiting for them to ask why my eyes were so green," he confesses.

Tammy laughs, and they embrace. Bruce tells her to hold on, runs out of the bedroom, and comes back with a Bible. They both start suggesting verses to each other about greed, contentment, envy. At first they just read some aloud to each other back and forth. Then they come to a particularly poignant passage somewhat by accident: "And Jesus said to [a follower], 'Foxes have holes, and birds of the air have nests, but the Son of Man has nowhere to lay his head'" (Luke 9:58).

They find themselves talking about how poor Jesus was compared to their own standard of living. Then they discuss His forty days in the wilderness, in danger from wild animals, with no food and absolutely no creature comforts. They talk about their queen bed with a pillow-top mattress, their thoroughly modern appliances, their wireless Internet, their cable television, their thermostat always set at 70 degrees. On and on they talk about the things they have. This leads them to think about another sermon they heard a year or so ago when their pastor said that everyone in the congregation was in the top 10 percent of the world's wealth. People all throughout India, Nepal, and the Dominican Republic would call their condo a palace. Tammy blushes as she thinks about her attitude toward Laura's opulent home.

They also remembered a sermon they heard this past Christmas Eve. *What was the passage for that message?* they think. After a while they find it: "For you know the grace of our Lord Jesus Christ, that though he was rich, yet for your sake he became poor, so that you by his poverty might become rich" (2 Corinthians 8:9).

Now the conversation focuses on their true riches. They remind each other that they are forgiven, free, saved, indwelt by God's Spirit, children of God, ambassadors for Christ, salt and light. On and on they talk about whom they are in Christ and just how much it cost their Savior to make these things happen.

After a while they get sleepy and a little more embarrassed. But just as they drift off to sleep, Tammy softly prays, "Thank you, Jesus. You gave everything you had for a spoiled brat like me."

"Amen," Bruce agrees. He turns off the light. The rest of the night is peaceful, with no more dreams of TVs. But there may have been one about an intergalactic trash compactor . . .

For Further Examination

1. Have you ever found yourself in a situation like Bruce and Tammy's? What was it? Did you also fake Christian "encouragement" too?

2. Why do you think that things like TVs and hardwood floors have such a strong effect on us so often?

3. Look back over the case study. Besides the Scriptures, there were many things that helped Bruce and Tammy get back on track after idolatry knocked them down. What were some of them?

4. What other passages could Bruce and Tammy have turned to for help?

Cherishing Christ More Than Stuff

Case #2: Sandra and Ashley against Unlimited Text Messaging

Patient Background: Sixteen-year-old dedicated Christian teen. She is fairly responsible for her age—a good student, involved in her church youth group, generally respectful of and obedient to her loving Christian parents. Like most teens, she enjoys an active social life. She lives with her parents and two younger siblings in a middle-class neighborhood in the suburbs.

Profile: Sandra, a forty-something mother of three, hasn't had to dig deep into her language skills for years. In college she was a double language major, French and Spanish, but her training has done little to help her translate the "hieroglyphics" on her daughter's cell phone screen. She knows that *lol* means "laugh out loud," but she is lost at making any sense out of *afaik* ("as far as I know"), *hth* ("hope that helps"), or *pos* ("parent over shoulder"). But right now Sandra is less concerned with the content of the texts—Ashley's a good kid. She has a genuine faith, is involved in her church youth group, and gets solid grades in school. Sandra is concerned with the *costs* of the texts.

"174 texts, Ashley?" her mother asks.

Sixteen-year-old Ashley has been waiting for this moment, and she has her answer prepared and even more polished than an attorney's closing argument.

"Mom, I know that's a lot. But Jane's parents just switched to an unlimited plan—they're saving a ton of money."

"Another way to save money is not to text 174 times in a week," Sandra retorts. "We pay five dollars a month for two hundred, Ashley. You only have twenty-six now for the rest of the month."

The conversation continues on—point/counterpoint—until Sandra starts to see the benefit of not worrying any more about overage charges. *It's only a few more dollars a month, after all,* she thinks. "I'll talk with your father about it," she concedes.

Her husband is fine with it. They aren't having any money troubles, and he will be glad to see his wife not fret over every cell phone bill that comes in the mail. So life goes on normally. A few extra bucks per month buy a lot of peace in the home, even though Ashley's heart has been breached, toppled, and now captured by an insidious idol.

Ashley cannot go anywhere without her Motorola. Oh, she's smart and knows how to conceal what has become an electronic appendage. Like many teens, she has mastered the art of texting under tables, blankets, coats—guiding her thumb over the keypad with scientific precision. But there are signs that she's beginning to crack.

She is distracted at the dinner table. Several family meals have ended with her parents sending her to her room for a flippant attitude.

"Ashley, you seem like you're on another planet. We just want to hear about your day," Sandra pleads.

"Mom, I told you—I've just got a lot on my mind right now. Sheesh!" Ashley barks.

Her father sends her to her room for disrespecting her mother. He thinks it's a good place for her to go and "collect her thoughts." She has no TV or computer in her room, but little does Dad know that she has a pocket-sized idol that's lighting up her world right now. Ashley retreats into her oasis and spends hours texting her friends about classes, favorite songs, and, of course, cute boys.

One day Sandra, who has become accustomed to barely glancing at the phone bill (just a brief smile at the unchanging monthly balance), decides to look over the call log. Last month, Ashley racked up 2,347 texts! *You've got to be kidding! Is that even possible?* Sandra wonders. She has been studying the subject of idolatry in her small group, and she doesn't need to give it a moment's thought. It is time for drastic action.

After a very unpleasant encounter, Sandra confiscates the Motorola. What has started out as protests—"Oh, come on, Mom. I'll cut back!"—now escalates to shouts and sobbing. "You're ruining my life, Mom!"

Sandra is composed. She stands her ground, even as Ashley runs into her room and slams the door. Then Sandra herself breaks. *How did I let my little girl get so enslaved to this stupid thing?*

After a few days, things settle down a bit. Ashley goes through a detox period of sorts, moody and withdrawn, but Sandra prays for her morning, noon, and night. One day, when things seem a little less tense, she takes her daughter out to Starbucks for lattes. Ashley is a bit reluctant at first, but once they are there, sipping caramel bliss, Ashley breaks.

"Mom, I know I've been a Tasmanian devil over this phone thing. I think it was killing me."

Sandra shows great restraint, revealing the slightest smile, but she's jumping for joy on the inside. The hold is beginning to break. Sandra talks with her daughter about last summer's youth retreat. Ashley remembers how joyful she had been when she got back home. "Mom, I just want to live full-out for Jesus," she had said. Sandra reminds her of the fact that she didn't even have a cell phone back then. Then she goes for broke: She decides to be vulnerable and tell her teenage daughter about a time in her life when she let something else rob her of the joy of cherishing Jesus more than anything. But that's another case study. For now, let's just enjoy the turning point: Ashley is beginning to see that stuff can really get in the way of a relationship with God.

For Further Examination

1. Have you, a family member, or friend, been attacked by an electronic idol of some sort—cell phone, computer, TV? Specifically, how did it get in the way of cherishing Christ above everything?

2. In Ashley's experience, at what point did a good gift (technology, convenience) become a god for her? How does this story illustrate the subtlety of idolatry?

3. Do you think Sandra or her husband showed poor judgment at any point in this story? What could they have done differently?

4. Do you think it is harder for teenagers today (compared to past generations) to treasure Christ above all else? How do you think churches, parents, and youth ministries can help kids get an all-consuming vision for Christ in such a stuff-saturated culture?

Cherishing Christ More Than Sex

Case #3: Sandra against Acceptance-Through-Sex

Patient Background: Forty-something married mom of three. Has been a Christian for more than twenty years. Extremely committed to Christ, church, and family. College educated, she speaks French and Spanish fluently. Like most of us, she has some lingering insecurities from her teenage years.

Profile: Ashley and Sandra find themselves at Starbucks just after the morning rush. The 10 a.m. sunshine is softly warming their quiet corner booth. Sandra knows that she can safely share her story.

"Ashley, I came back from a summer retreat when I was seventeen just like you did last year. I was ready to take on the world! It seemed that all I ever needed was my Bible and a place to pray. Jesus was enough. Then I met Jeff."

Ashley, who's known her dad for sixteen years, is pretty sure his name is not Jeff. She has never heard about this other man, and she intuitively knows that her mother is crossing an important threshold here. Their relationship is just about to take on a much deeper character. Ashley senses something sacred in the moment.

Sandra was a beautiful girl; at least that's what her parents always told her. But an unusually bad case of teen acne hid an otherwise beautiful face. Dermatologists, beauticians, and even a natural herb specialist were little able to help her. While she had caring parents and a few close friends who loved her unconditionally, high school was brutal. "Pizza Face," "Dartboard," and her personal favorite, "Pox," were everyday labels calloused kids threw her way. And though she knew that old "sticks-and-stones" saying, the names were hurting her—horribly.

"I often wondered how depressed I would have gotten had it not been for that summer camp," she tells Ashley.

"You mean the one where you became a Christian, Mom? You've told me about that, but . . ." Ashley looks down into her coffee cup a little sheepishly, "I don't think you ever mentioned a Jeff."

Fighting back tears more than twenty years after the fact, Sandra forces herself to smile, "Yes, I know, honey. It was a bittersweet summer."

The sweet part came at the start of a two-week Christian camp at an old ranch. Her friend Molly, one of those few close friends who didn't care about Sandra's acne, was a committed Christian. Up until that summer, Sandra had really liked Molly but simply tolerated her religious zeal. With some reluctance she went to the camp with her. It was there on the second day, at their nightly youth rally, that Sandra heard a simple message called "Jesus: Is He Your Treasure?" Everything seemed so clear to her: Jesus was a real person—the Son of God—and He gave his life for Sandra. It was the first time in years she didn't remember thinking about her acne for more than a few minutes. She was transfixed, awestruck, and then, quietly in her seat, she cried out to Jesus to save her.

The next several days were a honeymoon. She simply couldn't get enough of Jesus. Late night Bible talks with Molly, extended times of singing, and these really cool things called "prayer walks" filled her days and nights.

"To this day, "Sandra tells her daughter, "I don't know if I've ever experienced such a focused time of just being with Jesus. But it was gone as quickly as it came."

"I've got a feeling you're going to tell me about Jeff now," Ashley replies.

And she does. Now the bitter part. Jeff had just finished his senior year and was heading off to a Christian college in the fall.

Sandra hadn't even known there was such a thing as a Christian college. She was enthralled. Jeff was good-looking and funny, and he wanted to become a missionary. And here was the real shocker—he was totally into Sandra! The rest of that week Jeff was an integral part of those late night Bible talks, times of singing, and, yes, even her walking partner on those prayer treks. Sandra's faith was growing strong, but so was her affection for Jeff.

When camp ended, they each returned to their hometowns, which, sadly, were about an hour apart. But they spoke with each other every night, and they visited each other every weekend. By the end of the summer, Jeff started the hinting. "I just want to know that you'll still think about me when I'm away at school," he would say. "I wish I knew that you were really crazy about me."

Of course, Sandra protested. "How could you not know that, Jeff? I think I'm falling in love with you. I'll be crazy here with you so far away." The week before he went away, he played all of his cards. He wanted Sandra to sleep with him this coming weekend—their last weekend together before Thanksgiving.

And like so many similar stories, Sandra, who as a young Christian was pretty sure that this was wrong, would not please God, and would rob her of something sacred, just couldn't bear the thought of losing Jeff. Well . . . that was not entirely true. She couldn't stand losing his acceptance. That weekend came and went, but not before taking her innocence with it.

In the Starbucks, Ashley fights back tears of her own. She can see how hard this is for her mother to share, and she loves her now more than she's ever loved her. "Mom, he broke your heart, didn't he? He didn't want to see you again, did he?"

Sandra looks at her daughter interestingly—her pimple-free, even more beautiful daughter—and wants to protect her from all the evil in this world. She simply says, "No honey, he didn't. He got to college, wrote one letter, then never returned another letter or phone call again. Maybe he was ashamed, too. I never knew. But Ashley, I know what happens when something else, and that could be sex or even a stupid cell phone, becomes more precious to you than Christ. You've got to fight that, baby girl, whenever it sneaks up on you."

Ashley looks at her mom with affection so intense it almost hurts. She hasn't heard "baby girl" for years, but she doesn't mind one bit. Something beautiful has happened in this coffee shop this morning, something she prays she will never forget. By the grace of God, she won't.

For Further Examination

1. Sandra's story is all too common, isn't it? How much pressure do you think girls, even Christian girls, are under in our culture to have sex? What factors contribute to these pressures?

2. Do you think that Sandra was right to share this story with her sixteen-year-old daughter? Could telling an impressionable teen this story be potentially harmful? How can a parent be vulnerable without giving their teens license to sin?

3. In this story, was sex a different kind of idol for Sandra than it was for Jeff? How were their "sex idols" different?

4. Do you think that helping teens understand that premarital sex is a form of idolatry is a better approach than simply saying, "Premarital sex is a sin—don't do it?" Why or why not?

Cherishing Christ More Than Sex

Case #4: Bill against Pornography

Patient Background: Male, thirty-seven years old, commercial real-estate broker. Married, with three children. Financially successful, yet has a history of job terminations, which has meant several relocations for his family. Active in both church and social causes. Keeps a secret well, but not as well as he thinks . . .

Profile: A commercial real-estate broker, Bill has done rather well for himself. He and his wife, Susan, have an almost ridiculously picture-perfect life to the outside observer. A gorgeous five-bedroom colonial in one of the most picturesque neighborhoods, three beautiful children, and four (that's right—four) high-end cars in their driveway. Before you're tempted to label Bill a typical, rich American materialist, you should know that Bill sings in the choir in his church, has coordinated the annual Thanksgiving meal at a city homeless shelter, and currently serves as a big brother to two underprivileged kids who have no father. But Bill is also a committed idolater, and pornography is his god.

Two of his former employers reluctantly terminated his employment (remember, he's a great seller) for "repeated violations of the company's computer policy." Both companies had virtually identical protocols—no Internet gaming, gambling, or pornography. Bill could care less about Tetris and is too fiscally conservative for poker, but he is in love with his porn.

Bill will never forget the bile he felt rising in his throat as he desperately worked to conceal the truth from his wife. How would she ever understand? How could he put his family on the line for cheap thrills at his monitor? "Susan," just as he rehearsed, "they really can't afford what I'm worth anymore. They're in a catch-22. They like the money that I bring in, but they say I should find a firm that has the financial wherewithal to sustain a top broker."

In designing his cover-up, Bill has woefully underestimated his wife's smarts. Susan knows that her husband's explanation simply makes no sense, but she lets it go for now, half fearing what she might discover if she continues to pry. So off they move to another city after Bill comes home a week later with the most lucrative job offer he's ever gotten. He tells Susan that it's the chance of a lifetime, plus there's a great church in this new town—lots of ministry opportunity.

Today Bill finds himself on his six-month anniversary of his new job, in his new city, at his new desk, on his new computer, looking at his old porn. Just as he is about to click over to the next picture, an intrusive message blocks his screen: *"Access Denied!"* Bill is as frozen as his monitor. Forcing himself to slow his respirations, he thinks it through. *Could just be a glitch, right? Maybe the server went down in general? Maybe this has happened to everyone?* And even if this déjà vu moment proves to be incident #3, there will be a warning first. There has to be. Then he can really get his act together this time. He might even talk to one of his new pastors and tell him that he has "occasional struggles" with porn. Just as his self-reassurance starts to work its magic, George, his new boss, walks into his office.

"That's a bad habit you got there, Bill. Could get you fired, couldn't it?" George asks calmly.

The moment is surreal. Is George talking about Bill's coffee addiction? Bill is a bit of a java junkie. Hopefully that's all that George is highlighting. Just as he's about to respond, George continues.

"I.T. flagged you two weeks ago, Bill. I hoped it was just a fluke, but it appears that you are deep into this porn thing. I checked with your former employers—you know, the real top dogs there—not the best buddies that you listed on your references. But don't look so nervous, Bill. I'm not letting this happen. Here's how it's going to go down."

George proceeds to tell Bill that only a fool would let the top producer go over something like this. But as his supervisor, George can't allow his star broker to get caught in the web of company protocol, so Bill will simply have no more access to the Internet at work—ever. Any e-mails, downloading, other Internet tasks . . . will need to be done in George's office, under George's supervision.

On the drive home Bill tries to process whether this turn of events is a good thing. Keeping his job is good, but ruining his testimony with his boss isn't. Not having to tell Susan they're moving again is good, but not having ten to twelve hours of work Internet access a day isn't. Lately, Susan has been acting a little suspicious about his computer habits, so he's had to lay low on the home front. *Maybe the Lord has caught up with me*, he thinks. *Maybe it's time to truly give it up.* He ponders that thought for a few minutes, but the white noise of the surrounding traffic and the restlessness of his own thoughts seem to carry that question away.

In a few more minutes, he's pulling into an adult video store and thinking how easy it would be to watch DVDs on his laptop in his car. He snaps open his cell phone and tells Susan he has a late meeting and that he won't be home for a couple more hours.

By the time Bill pulls into his driveway, he feels dirtier and more ashamed than ever. In a moment of fierce resolve he takes the just-purchased DVDs out of his brief case and throws them in the trash can on the front walk. He enters his house feeling like he has beat this thing. *Lord, help me*, he prays. But later that night when his wife is sound asleep, he wakes up with the urge. He has to have his porn—now!

The night is foggy and a little chilly. Quietly he tiptoes to the front walk and carries the trashcan to the backyard. Before setting it down he trips on a stone, and the can flies out of his grasp. The bags within all burst as they hit the ground like water balloons. A neighbor's dog barks, and Bill holds his breath, waiting to see if a light in the house comes on. It never does. With relief Bill goes to work, digging through chicken bones, dirty diapers, coffee grounds, and other unidentified filth until his hands feel the familiar comfort of those thin DVD cases. His heart skips a beat as he rediscovers his "treasure." Then something incredible happens.

For a brief moment the fog and clouds about and above him disappear, and a brilliant shaft of moonlight falls directly on him. He sees himself, in his boxers, covered in trash, holding the movies like a kid on Christmas day holds a new toy, and he knows what he has become. Although he hasn't thought about this passage in years, it flashes across his mind with perfect clarity: *"Like a dog that returns to his vomit is a fool who repeats his folly."*

When is the last time he has cried over his sin? He can't remember. But then the dam breaks. Bill sobs on the dung heap of his addiction, at the altar of his idol. He goes on that way for some time. After a while he cleans up the mess, goes into his home and takes a very hot shower, then stays up all night on the couch reading the book of Proverbs. The next morning Susan wakes up early to find a teary-eyed Bill on the sofa.

"Honey?" she asks. "Didn't you have an early meeting at the office today?"

Bill stands, hugs his wife with an intensity that takes her by surprise, and finally, after all these years says, "We need to talk."

For Further Examination

1. Many men do not think that pornography is a serious problem. Why do you think they feel that way?

2. In Bill's case pornography cost him his job. What are some other things that pornography costs men?

3. What evidences of God's grace are found in this story?

4. How could understanding pornography as idol worship help men who battle it to stay pure? Read Proverbs 26:11 (the passage that Bill recalled at the end of the story) and think out loud about how this verse applies to other kinds of idolatry.

A First-Aid Kit
for Recovering Idolaters

"Hi, I'm Greg, and I'm an idolater."

If there were such a group as IA (Idolater's Anonymous), this is how I imagine myself making my weekly introduction. But what would I take from the group to help me in between meetings? What "steps" would I take to help me in my daily battle with addiction?

Now that you've finished reading about the idolatry syndrome and examined some case studies, you are hopefully more sensitive to the subtle pull and power of idolatry in your everyday experiences. As one recovering idolater to another, I'd like to invite you to take advantage of the resources below to fight your idols one day at a time. Consider it a sort of "first-aid kit" to help you when you've been sneak-attacked by idolatry's arrows.

I have divided this section into three categories: 1. our need for an awareness of idolatry's attacks; 2. the uselessness, danger, and wretchedness of idolatry; and 3. the incomparable beauty of Christ. Section 1 is designed to help you at all times, as a reminder that we can easily be lulled into thinking that we are not really in danger of falling into idolatry's clutches; it's actually more of a preventative tool than a first-aid help as we recognize our vulnerability to the attacks of the idolatry syndrome. Section 2 is aimed at enabling you to think clearly and critically about the emptiness and danger of things that seem fulfilling and innocuous. Section 3 serves as a window through which you can get a glimpse of the surpassing beauty of Jesus Christ, putting the puniness and pettiness of your idols in a proper light.

What should you do with this material? One thing is to understand that this information isn't just a first-aid kit that serves us once we've succumbed to idolatry. It's also like a vitamin, an offensive strategy, preventing us from getting "sick" in the first place. It's better to hide all of this in our heads and hearts now—so that we'll be better able to fight off the syndrome when it attacks. The problem with idolatry is that we may not realize that we've succumbed to it until we find ourselves in a vicious struggle. So do anything with this material that will help you go hard after adoring Christ and overthrowing your substitute saviors. Read, meditate, memorize, pray—anything to help you find your greatest satisfaction in Christ alone. God help you as you enter into His presence.

Our Need for an Awareness of Idolatry's Attacks

Scriptures

> The Lord said to Cain, "Why are you angry, and why has your face fallen? If you do well, will you not be accepted? And if you do not do well, sin is crouching at the door. Its desire is for you, but you must rule over it."
>
> Genesis 4:6–7

> Take care lest your heart be deceived, and you turn aside and serve other gods and worship them.
>
> Deuteronomy 11:16

And he said to them, "Take care, and be on your guard against all covetousness, for one's life does not consist in the abundance of his possessions."

Luke 12:15

See to it that no one takes you captive by philosophy and empty deceit, according to human tradition, according to the elemental spirits of the world, and not according to Christ.

Colossians 2:8

Take care, brothers, lest there be in any of you an evil, unbelieving heart, leading you to fall away from the living God.

Hebrews 3:12

Be sober-minded; be watchful. Your adversary the devil prowls around like a roaring lion, seeking someone to devour.

1 Peter 5:8

Quotes

Be on your guard. It's necessary to read the newspaper, but have you ever thought it's dangerous. It's necessary to watch television and go to the movies to understand what's going on in the world around us, but it's dangerous. Subtly, insidiously, the world can infiltrate into your life and squeeze you into its mold. So we need to be on our guard. The whole value system of the world can permeate our lives if we are not careful. Keep on your guard. Keep up your defenses. Maintain your critical faculties. Read the newspapers. Watch television, but do it critically.

—John Stott

If we are not watching and seeking the Lord's help in prayer, we often will not even notice temptation when it comes. When our spiritual eyes are shut or sleepy, we can fall more easily into sin.

—John MacArthur

When we have God's Word pure and clear, then we think ourselves all right; we become negligent, and repose in a vain security; we no longer pay due heed, thinking it will always so remain; we do not watch and pray against the devil, who is ready to tear the divine word out of hearts.

—Martin Luther

All kinds of alternative passions are making war on your soul every day to steal your faith and replace Christ with other treasures. Take care! Be on the look out! Be earnest! Be watchful over your heart. As Proverbs 4:23 says, "Watch over your heart with all diligence, for from it flow the springs of life."

—John Piper

Prayers

Search me, O God, and know my heart! Try me and know my thoughts! And see if there be any grievous way in me, and lead me in the way everlasting!

—Psalm 139:23–24

My Heavenly Father, I thank You, through Jesus Christ, Your beloved Son, that You kept me safe from all evil and danger last night. Save me, I pray, today as well, from every evil and sin, so that all I do and the way that I live will please you. I put myself in your care, body and soul and all that I have. Let

Your holy Angels be with me, so that the evil enemy will not gain power over me. Amen.

—Martin Luther, "A Morning Prayer"

Let me never forget that I am but a man of dust and ashes, a man with all the natural faults and passions that plague the race of men. I pray Thee, therefore, my Lord and Redeemer, save me from myself.

—A. W. Tozer

Try me, O God, and search the ground of my heart: prove me and examine my thoughts. Look well if there be any wickedness in me, any root of bitterness yet undiscovered; and lead me in the way everlasting. Show me the true state of my soul. Bring me out from every false refuge. Strip off every deceitful covering, every covering that is not of Thy Spirit. Forbid that the anchor of my hope should be cast, or the house of my dependence built, on any but Christ, the Rock of Ages.

—August Toplady

Prone to wander—Lord, I feel it—
Prone to leave the God I love;
Here's my heart—O take and seal it,
Seal it for they courts above.

—"Come, Thou Fount of Every Blessing"

The Uselessness, Danger, and Wretchedness of Idolatry

Scriptures

"I am the Lord your God, who brought you out of the land of Egypt, out of the house of slavery. You shall have no other gods before me. You shall not make for yourself a carved image, or any likeness of anything that is in heaven above, or that is in

the earth beneath, or that is in the water under the earth. You shall not bow down to them or serve them, for I, the Lord your God am a jealous God, visiting the iniquity of the fathers on the children to the third and the fourth generation of those who hate me."

Exodus 20:2–5

And do not turn aside after empty things that cannot profit or deliver, for they are empty.

1 Samuel 12:21

If I have made gold my trust or called fine gold my confidence, if I have rejoiced because my wealth was abundant or because my hand had found much, if I have looked at the sun when it shone, or the moon moving in splendor, and my heart has been secretly enticed, and my mouth has kissed my hand, this also would be an iniquity to be punished by the judges, for I would have been false to God above.

Job 31:24–28

Their idols are silver and gold, the work of human hands. They have mouths, but do not speak; eyes, but do not see. They have ears, but do not hear; noses, but do not smell. They have hands, but do not feel; feet, but do not walk; and they do not make a sound in their throat. Those who make them become like them; so do all who trust in them.

Psalm 115:4–8

Has a nation changed its gods, even though they are no gods? But my people have changed their glory for that which does not profit. Be appalled O heavens, at this; be shocked, be utterly desolate, declares the Lord.

Jeremiah 2:11–12

*If anyone else thinks he has reason for confidence in the flesh,
I have more: circumcised on the eighth day, of the people of
Israel, of the tribe of Benjamin, a Hebrew of Hebrews; as to
the law, a Pharisee; as to zeal, a persecutor of the church; as
to righteousness, under the law blameless. But whatever gain
I had, I counted as loss for the sake of Christ. Indeed, I count
everything as loss because of the surpassing worth of knowing
Christ Jesus my Lord. For his sake I have suffered the loss all
things and count them as rubbish, in order that I may gain
Christ.*

Philippians 3:4–8

Quotes

There is nothing so abominable in the eyes of God and of
men as idolatry, whereby men render to the creature that
honor which is due only to the Creator.

—Blaise Pascal

My sin was this, that not in him but in his creatures—myself
and others—I sought for pleasures, honors, and truths, and
so fell headlong into sorrows, confusions, errors.

—Augustine

The idolatrous heart assumes that God is other than He
is—in itself a monstrous sin—and substitutes for the true
God one made after its own likeness. Always this God will
conform to the image of the one who created it and will be
base or pure, cruel or kind, according to the moral state of
the mind from which it emerges.

—A. W. Tozer

It is truly said that "they are no gods," for the objects of our foolish love are very doubtful blessings, the solace which they yield us now is dangerous, and the help which they can give us in the hour of trouble is little indeed. Why, then, are we so bewitched with vanities? We pity the poor heathen who adore a god of stone, and yet worship a god of gold. Where is the vast superiority between a god of flesh and one of wood? The principle, the sin, the folly is the same in either case, only that in ours the crime is more aggravated because we have more light, and sin in the face of it. The heathen bows to a false deity, but the true God he has never known; we commit two evils, inasmuch as we forsake the living God and turn unto idols. May the Lord purge us all from this grievous iniquity!

—Charles Spurgeon

Prayers

The dearest idol I have known,
Whatever that idol be,
Help me to tear it from thy throne,
And worship only thee

—William Cowper

Eternal God, in whom we live and move and have our being, whose face is hidden from us by our sins, and whose mercy we forget in the blindness of our hearts: cleanse us from all our offenses, and deliver us from proud thoughts and vain desires, that with reverent and humble hearts we may draw near to you, confessing our faults, confiding in your grace, and finding in you our refuge and strength; through Jesus Christ your Son.

—Book of Common Worship

I am utterly ashamed that I am what I am in myself; I have no green shoot in me nor fruit, but thorns and thistles; I am a fading leaf that the wind drives away; I live bare and barren as a winter tree, unprofitable, fit to be hewn down and burnt. Lord, dost Thou have mercy on me?

Thou hast struck a heavy blow at my pride, at the false god of self, and I lie in pieces before Thee. But Thou hast given me another master and lord, Thy Son, Jesus, and now my heart is turned towards holiness, my life speeds as an arrow from a bow towards complete obedience to Thee. Help me in all my doings to put down sin and to humble pride. Save me from the love of the world and the pride of life, from everything that is natural to fallen man, and let Christ's nature be seen in me day by day. Grant me grace to bear Thy will without repining, and delight to be not only chiseled, squared, or fashioned, but separated from the old rock where I have been embedded so long, and lifted from the quarry to the upper air, where I may be built in Christ for ever.

—The Valley of Vision

The Imcomparable Beauty of Christ

Scriptures

Behold my servant, whom I uphold, my chosen, in whom my soul delights; I have put my Spirit upon him; he will bring forth justice to the nations.

Isaiah 42:1

A voice from heaven said, "This is my beloved Son, with whom I am well pleased."

Matthew 3:17

I am the good shepherd. The good shepherd lays down his life for the sheep. He who is a hired hand and not a shepherd, who does not own the sheep, sees the wolf coming and leaves the sheep and flees, and the wolf snatches them and scatters them. He flees because he is a hired hand and cares nothing for the sheep. I am the good shepherd. I know my own and my own know me, just as the Father knows me and I know the Father; and I lay down my life for the sheep.

John 10:11–15

For you know the grace of our Lord Jesus Christ, that though he was rich, yet for your sake he became poor, so that you by his poverty might become rich.

2 Corinthians 8:9

He is the image of the invisible God, the firstborn of all creation. For by him all things were created, in heaven and on earth, visible and invisible, whether thrones or dominions or rulers or authorities—all things were created through him and for him. And he is before all things, and in him all things hold together. And he is the head of the body, the church. He is the beginning, the firstborn from the dead, that in everything he might be preeminent. For in him all the fullness of God was pleased to dwell, and through him to reconcile to himself all things, whether on earth or in heaven, making peace by the blood of his cross.

Colossians 1:15–20

[The Son] is the radiance of the glory of God and the exact imprint of his nature, and he upholds the universe by the word of his power. After making purification for sins, he sat down at the right hand of the Majesty on high.

Hebrews 1:3

And they sang a new song, saying, "Worthy are you to take the scroll and to open its seals, for you were slain, and by your blood you ransomed people for God from every tribe and language and people and nation.

Revelation 5:9

Quotes

The Maker of man became man that He, Ruler of the stars, might be nourished at the breast; that He, the Bread, might be hungry; that He, the Fountain, might thirst; that He, the Light, might sleep; that He, the Way, might be wearied by the journey; that He, the Truth, might be accused by false witnesses; that He, the Judge of the living and the dead, might be brought to trial by a mortal judge; that He, Justice, might be condemned by the unjust; that He, Discipline, might be scourged with whips; that He, the Foundation, might be suspended upon a cross; that Courage might be weakened; that Security might be wounded; that Life might die.

To endure these and similar indignities for us, to free us, unworthy creatures, He who existed as the Son of God before all ages, without a beginning, deigned to become the Son of Man in these recent years. He did this although He who submitted to such great evils for our sake had done no evil and although we, who were the recipients of so much good at His hands, had done nothing to merit these benefits.

—Augustine

We admire him for his glory, but even more because his glory is mingled with humility. We admire him for his uncompromising justice, but even more because it is tempered with mercy. We admire him for his majesty, but even more because it is a majesty in meekness. We love the way he stumped the proud scribes with his wisdom, and we love it even more because he could be simple enough to love children and spend time with them.

—John Piper

Suppose I am in England; there is abundance of water and I cannot sell it; water is so common, and therefore so cheap. But put a man in the desert and let the water-skin be dried up, let him come to the well wherein he expected to find water, and it has failed him; can you not conceive that that small drop of water might be worth a king's ransom? Nay, that a man might hoard it up, and conceal it from all his comrades, because on that small drop of water depended his life? The way to prize water is to value it with a tongue like a firebrand, and with a mouth like an oven. Then can I estimate its value when I know its worth. So with Christ. The worldly man does not care for Christ, because he has never hungered and thirsted after him; but the Christian is athirst for Christ; he is in a dry and thirsty land, where not water is, and his heart and his flesh pant after God, yea for the living God; and as the thirsty soul dying, cries out water, water, water, so the Christian cries out Christ, Christ, Christ! This is the one thing needful for me, and if I have it not, this thirst must destroy me.

—Charles Spurgeon

Christ is the very essence of all delights and pleasures, the very soul and substance of them. As all the rivers are gathered into the ocean, which is the meeting-place of all the waters in the world, so Christ is that ocean in which all true delights and pleasures meet.

—John Flavel

He is a portion that exactly, and directly suits—
The condition of the soul,
The desires of the soul,
The necessities of the soul,
The wants of the soul,
The longings of the soul,
And the prayers of the soul,
The soul can crave nothing, nor wish for
Nothing, but what is to be found in Christ.
He is light to enlighten the soul,
Wisdom to counsel the soul,
Power to support the soul,
Goodness to supply the soul,
Mercy to pardon the soul,
Beauty to delight the soul,
Glory to ravish the soul,
And fullness to fill the soul.

—Thomas Brooks

Jesus Christ, the condescension of divinity, and the exaltation of humanity.

—Phillips Brooks

Prayers

Turn your eyes upon Jesus,
Look full in His wonderful face,
And the things of earth will grow strangely dim
In the light of His glory and grace.

—Helen H. Lemmel

Come, my Way, my Truth, my Life!
Such a Way as gives us breath,
Such a Truth as ends all strife,
Such a Life as killeth death.

—George Herbert

Thanks be to thee, O Lord Jesus Christ, for all the benefits
which Thou hast given us; for all the pains and insults which
Thou hast borne for us. O most merciful redeemer, friend and
brother, may we know thee more clearly, love thee more dearly
and follow thee more nearly, for thine own sake.

—St. Richard of Chichester

Help me to be less pleased with my spiritual experiences, and
when I feel at ease after sweet communings, teach me it is far
too little I know and do. Blessed Lord, let me climb up near to
Thee, and love, and long, and plead, and wrestle with Thee,
and pant for deliverance from the body of sin, for my heart is
wandering and lifeless, and my soul mourns to think it should
ever lose sight of its beloved. Wrap my life in divine love, and
keep me ever desiring Thee, always humble and resigned to
Thy will, more fixed on Thyself, that I may be more fitted for
doing and suffering.

—The Valley of Vision

Jesus, priceless treasure,
Source of purest pleasure,
Truest friend to me,
Long my heart was burning,
And my soul was yearning,
Lord, with you to be!
Yours I am, O spotless Lamb;
Nothing I'll allow to hide you,
Nothing ask beside you.

In your arms I rest me;
Foes who would molest me
Cannot reach me here.
Though the earth be shaking,
Every heart be quaking,
Jesus calms my fear.
Sin and hell in conflict fell
With their bitter storms assail me;
Jesus will not fail me.

Satan, I defy you;
Death, I now decry you;
Fear, I bid you cease.
World, you cannot harm me
Nor your threats alarm me.
While I sing of peace.
God's great power guards every hour;
Earth and all its depths adore him,
Silent bow before him.

Hence, all earthly treasure!
Jesus is my pleasure,

Jesus is my choice.
Hence, all empty glory!
What to me your story
Told with tempting voice?
Pain or loss or shame or cross
Shall not from my Savior move me
Since he chose to love me.

Hence, all fears and sadness,
For the Lord of gladness,
Jesus, enters in.
Those who love the Father,
Though the storms may gather,
Still have peace within.
For, whatever I must bear,
Still in you lies purest pleasure,
Jesus, priceless treasure!

—Johann Franck

Come, Lord Jesus!

—Revelation 22:20

Recommended Reading

Lydia Brownback, *Contentment: A Godly Woman's Adornment* (Crossway, 2008). I have yet to talk with a woman who hasn't loved this devotional. Brownback helps women look to Christ for their ultimate satisfaction.

Kris Lundgaard, *Through the Looking Glass* (P&R, 2000). A "best-kept secret" among Christian books. Lundgaard does a masterful job of helping the reader ponder the beauty and majesty of Christ. An outstanding devotional book.

David McCasland, *Oswald Chambers: Abandoned to God* (Discovery House, 1993). This award-winning biography is absolutely riveting. It tells the story of the man behind what may be the most famous daily devotional, *My Utmost for His Highest*. Chambers' life is an almost epic story of seeking to cherish Christ above everything.

John Piper, *Desiring God* (Multnomah, 2003). In his signature work, Piper unpacks one of the most helpful insights given to the church in the last century. "God is most glorified in us when we are most satisfied in Him." This book is a clarion call for all those interested in cherishing Christ more than anything.

John Piper, *Seeing and Savoring Jesus Christ* (Crossway, 2004). A tiny book, but even if it is the only book you can purchase all year, buy it! Provocative reflections on why Jesus is precious to the believer.

Charles Spurgeon, *Morning and Evening* (Whitaker House, 2001). One would be hard pressed to find a better daily devotional that fans the flames of devotion to Christ. Having stood the test of time, this nineteenth-century British preacher has helped countless Christians wake up and fall asleep to glorious thoughts of Jesus.

John Stott, *The Cross of Christ* (IVP, 1986). It has become my habit to read this book once a year. Stott's exposition of what Jesus accomplished for us in His death is both profound and practical. He writes, "The Cross is a blazing fire at which the flame of our love is kindled, but we have to get near enough for its sparks to fall on us."

Ed Welch, *Addictions: A Banquet in the Grave* (P&R, 2001). One of the few resources available that handles the issue of addiction in a sensitive yet thoroughly biblical way. Chockfull of practical application and illustration, this is a must-read for the person who wants to consider the relationship between idolatry and addiction.

Note to the Reader

The publisher invites you to share your response to the message of this book by writing Discovery House Publishers, Box 3566, Grand Rapids, MI 49501, USA. For information about other Discovery House books, music, or videos, contact us at the same address or call 1-800-653-8333. Find us on the Internet at http://www.dhp.org/ or send e-mail to books@dhp.org.